IFLA

International Federation of Library Associations and Institutions
Fédération Internationale des Associations de Bibliothécaires et des Bibliothèques
Internationaler Verband der bibliothekarischen Vereine und Institutionen
Международная Федерация Библиотечных Ассоциаций и Учреждений
Federación Internacional de Asociaciones de Bibliotecarios y Bibliotecas

IFLA Publications 69

Global Perspectives on Preservation Education

by Michèle Valerie Cloonan

K · G · Saur
München · New Providence · London · Paris 1994

IFLA Publications
edited by Carol Henry

Recommended catalog entry:

Global Perspectives on Preservation Education / by
Michèle Valerie Cloonan under the auspices of the
IFLA PAC Core Programme
München, New Providence, London, Paris: K.G. Saur, 1994
X, 109 p 21 cm
(IFLA Publications: 69)
ISBN 3-598-21796-X

Die Deutsche Bibliothek – CIP-Einheitsaufnahme

Global perspectives on preservation education / [International
Federation of Library Associations and Institutions]. Ed. by
Michèle Valerie Cloonan. - München ; New Providence ;
London ; Paris : Saur, 1994
(IFLA publications : 69)
ISBN 3-598-21796-X
NE: Cloonan, Michèle Valerie [Hrsg.]; International Federation of
Library Associations and Institutions: IFLA publications

∞

Printed on acid-free paper
The paper used in this publication meets the minimum requirements of American National
Standard for Information Sciences – Permanence of Paper for Printed Library Materials,
ANSI Z39.48-1984.

Druck / Printed by Strauss Offsetdruck GmbH, Mörlenbach
Binden / Bound by Buchbinderei Schaumann, Darmstadt

ISBN 3-598-21796-X
ISSN 0344-6891 (IFLA Publications)

Table of Contents

This Work is Dedicated to

Christopher Charles Mann

1956 - 1992

Preface

Time over the roofs of what has nearly been
Circling, a migratory, static bird,
Predicts no change in future's lancing shape,
And daylight shows the streets still tangled up;
Time points the simian camera in the head
Upon confusion to be seen and seen.
(Philip Larkin, *Disintegration*, 3rd stanza)

In 1991 I was selected as one of the Vosper Programme Fellows. For my project I proposed to undertake a study of preservation education in library schools and other institutions in order to determine current and possible future directions of this field. Based on my findings I had planned to draft a model programme for preservation education that could be implemented in library schools. I gathered my data through questionnaires, interviews, and extensive reading.

Since undertaking this project, however, a number of events have occurred which have affected my perspectives on preservation education. As a result, this document is different from the one I had originally envisioned writing. Rather than design a model educational programme for library schools, I have taken a more general approach and made broad-based recommendations. This is because it has become clear that library schools in the United States will continue to be threatened with closure or downsizing, in part due to the retrenchment under way in most universities. Since that is the case, we must continue to explore the full range of educational opportunities in preservation.

Changes in past and current educational practices are examined in light of other societal changes. (I have described changes in American practices for my examples because I am more familiar with those than I am with practices in other countries.) These changes include political transformations; shifting institutional structures; new technologies which allow for different methods of disseminating information; and funding approaches.

There are different perspectives on these changes; they are represented throughout this report by the comments of the people whom I interviewed. Some of them requested that I not quote them directly because they did not want their own views to be mistakenly identified as the views of the institutions for which they work. For consistency I decided not to reveal the source of any of the quotes. Instead, I have included a list of the interviewees in Appendix A, and I also acknowledge information gleaned through interviews with parenthetical citations.

This study has itself been profoundly affected by change. My research began in 1991 at the IFLA Conference in Moscow. I conducted my first interview with Susan Swartzburg in our Hotel Metropol room during the Putsch. We pondered not only about changes in the field of preservation, but about new directions for what was then still the Soviet Union. Our last night in Moscow, we watched the statue of Sverdlov come down like a curtain after the final act. Those remarkable days set the tone for this report, which I have written in the midst of profound changes in my own institution.

I had hoped to interview a number of people at that IFLA conference. The Russian librarians were preoccupied with running a conference amidst the Putsch while other potential interviewees left the conference early. So I interviewed as many people as I could, though everyone was distracted by events at the nearby Russia House, where Boris Yeltsin was in captivity. (One interviewee, who was staying in the same hotel as the Russian army, was in his room while it was broken into just hours before our interview.)

But the Russian Putsch was only the first of several events of the past two years which remind us of the continuing volatility—both man-made and natural—in all parts of the world. Since August 1991 civil wars have escalated in countries such as the former Yugoslavia; one of the worst riots in American history occurred in Los Angeles in April 1992; Hurricane Andrew struck Florida in September 1992; and a terrorist bomb exploded outside the Uffizi Gallery in May 1993. An agricultural archive, the Accademia dei Georgofili, the oldest such archive in the world and part of the Uffizi complex, was nearly destroyed (Havemann, "'Mafia Terror' Blamed in Blast," A1; Cowell, "Bombing in Florence," A7). All of these events resulted in the destruction of library materials and/or works of art, reminding us that caring for our cultural heritage will always be a difficult endeavor. The juxtaposition of destruction and restoration was well illustrated during the August 1991 IFLA conference in Russia. In Moscow we witnessed cherry-pickers removing the statues of communist leaders. By the end of the week, all of the statue bases were spray-painted. Then, in St. Petersburg, Susan Swartzburg and I saw the painstaking restoration work in St. Catherine's Palace, efforts which have been going on since after the Germans retreated from Russia at the end of World War II. Cycles of destruction and renewal are perpetual for artifacts, as they are for life itself.

In addition to the political upheavals of the past two years, we have experienced educational upheavals as well. Many American universities are more concerned about becoming effective "cost centers" than with retaining excellent academic programs. Library schools tend to be small units on university campuses, and they do not generate the large income that business and law schools do. The two library schools in the University of California system—Berkeley and UCLA—have been threatened with disestablishment. Though it now appears that both programs will survive, they will do so with greatly diminished resources. Universities in the United States are going through a period of retrenchment—and this time it probably will be permanent rather than temporary, as it was in the 1970s. Thus this report will re-evaluate the role of the university in preservation education.

Whereas twenty years ago we placed many expectations on governmental institutions, recent events have made it only too clear that future educational activities around the world are going to become more decentralized. Changes in the global economy coupled with new communication technologies have pushed us into decentralization. But new technologies will also aid us in the rapid dissemination of information. These issues, and how they relate to preservation education, will be discussed at length in chapter 3, "International Preservation Strategies" and chapter 7, "Dissemination of Information."

As this decade progresses, international associations such as IFLA will become more crucial in the dissemination of information. Monetary resources may be decreasing, but the variety of communication resources is increasing, as is the need and desire for more cooperative activities. We must focus on how best to take advantage of these new opportunities.

Acknowledgments

This work was supported by the International Federation of Library Associations (IFLA) and the Council on Library Resources (CLR) under the auspices of the Robert Vosper IFLA Fellows Programme. The University of California at Los Angeles also supported this research by providing me with part-time research assistants during the academic years 1991-1993: Diane Barrie, Ann Williams, Teresa Lupe Grenot, Janet Shiban, and Lenora Shull. These five spent countless hours hunting down elusive citations, arranging interviews, deciphering questionnaires, and so on.

Susan G. Swartzburg, my first interviewee, deserves special thanks. Her generosity and enthusiasm are unparalleled.

Josephine R. Fang has been a beacon for international preservation education and a wonderful resource for me. For her tireless work, I would like to give her special thanks.

I would like to thank the other individuals who filled out my questionnaires, or who were interviewed in person or on the phone. The interviews in particular led to many stimulating discussions and provided me with new insights. Two interviewees in particular were generous with their resources: Ellen McCrady (Abbey Publications) and Merrily Smith (Library of Congress).

Karen Goff, of the West Virginia Library Commission, provided access to some of the UNESCO Ramp Studies.

Finally, thanks to my two most important mentors: Marguerite Bouvard (ma tante), and Sidney E. Berger (my husband).

1. The Context for Preservation Education

> Above and beyond their specialized . . . training, . . . preservationists must also be generalists. That is, they must see their own special area of expertise as being only one strand in a larger fabric, the warp and woof of which consist of many other coequal and coexistent specialties. (Fitch, 1990, p. xiv.)

The complexity of the care of objects "in the larger fabric" of our world is illustrated by the various phrases which we use to describe objects. The terms *cultural property, cultural patrimony,* and *national treasures*, for example, represent concepts that are antithetical to some ways of thinking—some might even characterize these terms as colonialist because they emerged from the tradition of one culture claiming ownership of the artifacts of another.

The tribal perspective of some Native American Indians holds that we are keepers of our own treasures. The very term *preservation* seems, to some, to suggest that culture is not a living thing. Native Americans are not concerned solely with objects; they are also concerned with the retention (preservation) of the Native American ways of life: language, traditional uses of land, sacred places and rituals, and oral history. The term *guardianship*, on the other hand, implies that we will care for objects, though we do not necessarily own them. Therefore, some prefer *guardianship* to the more all-encompassing term *preservation*. (Interviews with Cheryl Metoyer-Duran, 2/17/93 and 12/6/93.)

Cultures also hold different philosophical and religious beliefs which may dictate the ways in which objects are used. In Jewish tradition there is a differentiation between holy objects and other ritual objects. Sacred laws dictate the manufacture, use, handling, repair, and even the disposal of holy objects such as the *Torah* (Greene, Ray).

These examples illustrate that the preservation of cultural treasures has led different societies to care for objects in different ways. The care provided has stemmed not only from philosophical and religious beliefs, but from the available resources of a given country or nation at a given time. Sometimes religious beliefs stemmed from practical necessities. For example, some of the kosher laws were based on the realities of desert living before refrigeration. Even today our ideas about conservation and preservation arise from certain beliefs (e.g., that we should save as much as possible from all cultures); aesthetics (that there are certain ways in which objects should appear); and the available technologies (preservation microfilming, mass deacidification, etc.). In a hundred years, the philosophic, aesthetic, and technological aspects of our preservation practices will be evaluated just as we have evaluated the practices of those who worked a hundred years ago.

While there may be no universal concept of preservation, there may be particular features of the broader notion that it may be useful to mention. For example, every culture saves something of its past, whether physical objects, religious or social rituals, moral customs, or habitats (Though to preserve habitats one must recognize the inherent changes brought about by weathering. *See* Mostafavi and Leatherbarrow, *On Weathering*, pp. 6, 116, 120.) Also, there might be some similar motives among cultures for preservation.

Another feature of the broad notion of preservation is the idea that people believe they can benefit in one way or another by exposure to, familiarity with, and knowledge and understanding of items or beliefs of the past. Embedded in this notion is the sense of utility in this knowledge-a utility that we can pass on to our offspring. The knowledge we gain is a form of power. In fact, one notion is that saving another culture's artifacts gives the preservers some measure of control over the other culture. So while it may be that there is no universal definition of preservation, some common threads lie at the root of all attempts to preserve the past.

** *** ** *** **

This report will necessarily reflect western biases since that is the background of the author and most of her sources. However, I will try to offer as broad a perspective as possible.

We must all be humble rather than chauvinistic when thinking about preserving the treasures of this world. Any recommendations must be tempered by the cultural or political circumstances of different countries or regions of the world. And we must always be sensitive to the various connotations of the term *preservation*.

** *** ** *** **

What are the origins of conservation and preservation education?

Techniques for conservation have grown out of the methods used for creating artifacts. These methods were learned in the course of apprenticeships. European Medieval scribes prepared the surfaces of vellum for writing and they also mixed their own inks. With so much knowledge of the materials used to create books, they could also repair their manuscripts. (This tradition is carried on today by *sofers,* the Jewish scribes who create and repair *Torahs.*) Similarly, painters who ground their own pigments and prepared their painting surfaces could also repair damaged works. By the high Renaissance artists had at their disposal a handbook, *Il Libro dell'Arte*, written by Cennino d'Andrea Cennini in the 15th century, which offered information on most aspects of drawing, painting, and illuminating. For all practical purposes, the training for a scribe or a painter was also the training for a conservator.

The system of artisan as repairer of damaged materials worked well enough when the materials themselves were durable. As materials became less durable, and as more causes of deterioration emerged during the industrial revolution, preservation became more complex. One might argue, for example, that the history of paper is the history of a product which has qualitatively declined over the centuries. The introduction of the Hollander beater in the seventeenth century which macerated the rag fibers, poor sources of water, and the introduction of chlorine bleach in the late 18th century, all led to the deterioration of paper. (All these "innovations" took place even before the introduction of alum-rosin sizing and wood-pulp into paper manufacture!) The resulting chemical deterioration of paper was beyond the skills of a craftsman to remedy.

By the end of the eighteenth century scholars attempted to use scientific methods to determine the causes of and treatments for fading writing inks. In the nineteenth century, the English chemist Michael Faraday analyzed foreign printing papers for William Savage to determine the reason for their desirable qualities, " . . . in order to prod English papermakers into duplicating these" (Abt, 25-26). Numerous articles and books were written in the nineteenth century about the deterioration of paper, but neither the research nor the writing of the period led to the development of formal conservation training programs. This is not surprising; the apprenticeship system was the predominant source of training for all professions until well into the twentieth century, and, in the case of conservation, it focused more on the originating craft than on the treatment of the products of that craft.

The next stage in the development of "conservation" education took place in museums and libraries, though the institutional approach did not replace the apprenticeship system, a system still in existence. Examples of early museum and library training programs in the United States can be found in the Fogg Art Museum and the Newberry Library.

In the United States, the shift towards the university as a setting for art conservation education can be traced to the establishment of the Conservation Center of the Institute of Fine Arts at New York University in 1960; it was the first graduate-level training program in the United States. Sheldon Keck became its first director in 1961 (Sack, "In Memoriam," 19). The second graduate program in conservation was started in 1969 by Sheldon and Caroline Keck in Cooperstown, New York, under the auspices of the State University of New York and the New York State Historical Association. (This program is now at Buffalo State College.) Several years later a third graduate program was started at the University of Delaware. To date, these are the only three graduate programs in art conservation in the United States.

Recognizing that the conservation of library materials required somewhat different training from that needed for art conservation, Paul Banks began, in the late 1970s, to examine the possibility of establishing an analogous graduate training program in a library school. In a 1979 *Library Journal* article, he wrote, "There are . . . some fundamental differences between library conservation and most aspects of museum conservation; library conservation involves, in addition to treatment of individual items of high value, mass problems" (Banks, "Education," 1014). His work resulted in the formation of two programs at the School of Library Service at Columbia University in 1980-81: one in preservation administration and one in conservation. Although Banks at that time did not formally differentiate between the terms "conservation" and "preservation," a co-creator of the Columbia programs, Pamela Darling, did (Darling, "Creativity," and "To the Editor"). Since the 1980s, spurred on by both Darling's writings and the formation of the Columbia programs, Americans have used *conservation* to refer to the physical treatment of individual items, and *preservation* as a more general term pertaining to collections as a whole having to do with administering programs: disaster recovery plans, patron education, reformatting, cooperative initiatives, library binding and other physical treatments, and mass treatments, such as mass deacidification. So conservation is sometimes an integral part of a comprehensive preservation program.

This report touches on aspects of conservation, but is primarily concerned with preservation education.

Preservation Education in American Library Schools

Although the School of Library Service at Columbia was the only library school in the United States to offer certificates in conservation and preservation administration (these programs are now at the University of Texas at Austin), other American library schools have offered preservation specializations. The first such classes were taught in the early 1970s by Paul Banks (University of Illinois) and George Cunha (University of Rhode Island) (Cloonan, "Preservation Education," 188). As the number of preservation positions advertised in library journals increased in the 1980s (Cloonan/Norcott, "Evolution," 651), there is anecdotal evidence that the number of library schools offering preservation courses also increased. I estimate (based on a perusal of my preservation education files) that thirty ALA-accredited library schools are presently offering elective courses in preservation. Elements of preservation curricula are listed in Table D.

Although thirty may seem like a high number, it is important to point out that at many American library schools the preservation course is taught by an adjunct who may teach at night or on weekends, sometimes off campus. Therefore, the adjunct may not even know the full-time faculty, and probably has not had any role in the development of the curriculum. I believe that in order for preservation to be a significant part of a library degree program, it must be integrated into the core curriculum. If preservation is offered only as an elective, then only a few students will learn about it. Of the thirty library schools offering preservation courses, I estimate that only twelve have integrated preservation into the core curriculum.

There is another problem inherent in preservation education in American library schools that is more daunting than the elective versus core curriculum issue: the survival of American library school programs. In the last decade, the programs at Columbia, Case-Western, Emory, Chicago, Northern Illinois, Minnesota, Denver, Oregon, USC, and Brigham Young have closed, and the programs at UCLA and Berkeley have been threatened. It looks, as of this writing, that UCLA and Berkeley will survive, but that they will be down-sized and/or merged with other schools. In such an environment, how well is preservation education served? This issue will be considered in Chapters 2 and 8.

With the increasing recognition of the potential loss of millions of volumes of paper-based books, and the proliferation of impermanent electronic formats, library schools should require the introduction of preservation issues into core, required courses. And even if universities are forced to close their library schools, they should maintain preservation as part of the curriculum in another department.

Preservation Education in the United Kingdom
The Ratcliffe Report

In 1984 The British Library published a report by F.W. Ratcliffe, *Preservation Policies and Conservation in British Libraries*, which revealed not only the lack of resources applied to preservation in libraries, but also the dearth of preservation courses in library schools, and the lack of preservation information available to library staff. One result of the Ratcliffe Report (as it has come to be called) was that the Library Association organized a seminar in 1986 on "Education for Preservation." One of the outcomes of the seminar was the agreement among library schools that the teaching of specialist conservator skills was outside the purview of library schools, but that the teaching of preservation as a whole was not (Clements, "Preservation and Library School," 136). Whether this exclusion of the teaching of conservation from library schools is justifiable remains to be seen. In chapter 3 we will see that in some parts of the world such as Africa, hands-on courses are seen as vital to the library school curriculum.

Today several library schools in the British Isles have preservation management courses in their curricula, including the University of Northumbria, Loughborough University, and University College London, to name just a few (interviews with and/or questionnaires from Day, Feather, Foot, McIlwaine).

Another result of the Ratcliffe report was that the British Library established the National Preservation Office which disseminates information throughout the British Isles.

John Feather is currently working on an update to the Ratcliffe Report. His update will evaluate the preservation initiatives undertaken since the Report and recommend future strategies (interview with Feather, 8/3/92).

Preservation Education in Library Schools Outside Britain and the U.S.

There is also some activity in library schools outside of Britain and the United States. This will be discussed in chapter 3, "International Preservation Strategies."

Other Preservation Education Opportunities in the United States

In the United States, library schools have not been the only providers of preservation education—in fact some might argue that library schools are not even the most important providers. Professional associations, regional centers, regional networks, the Library of Congress, the National Archives, and other large libraries and archives have sponsored workshops, courses, publications, etc. (Table A). Some of these opportunities have served practicing librarians better than have library schools. Why is this so?

Library schools in the United States are found in universities of all types. Different universities have different mandates. Some, like the University of California, have never been seriously interested in extension programs or continuing education for professionals. Other schools such as Kent State University and Rutgers the State University of New Jersey, have made a strong commitment to continuing education. In 1990-91 Rutgers began to offer a Professional Development Certificate in Preservation (interview with Swartzburg, 8/19/91).

But the program at Rutgers is unique; most librarians supplement their preservation training at the types of organizations listed above. Therefore, in recommending future strategies for preservation education, one must evaluate opportunities in a variety of settings.

In the twentieth century preservation education has gradually evolved from a hands-on apprenticeship served under a master bookbinder to a management-oriented discipline where a master's degree in librarianship and sometimes also an advanced certificate comprise the training. Conservation has evolved into a more scientific, item-oriented discipline. (Though conservators are also interested in issues that relate to the collections as a whole such as environmental monitoring, and protective enclosures.) Conservation training programs include internships, a vestige of the apprenticeship system, and require not only that students possess manual dexterity but also a background in chemistry. In the United States, the programs are also at the master's level.

In addition to educational opportunities in library schools, librarians can benefit from workshops offered by library associations, regional centers or regional networks, or internships in libraries with well established preservation programs.

As we come to the end of the century, new sources for education are also emerging through electronic networks and the collaborative efforts of different types of institutions (Table B). The objective of this study is twofold: to explore the variety of educational opportunities now available or soon to be so, and to discuss the recommendations of the people whom I interviewed. The evaluation of opportunities and recommendations should help IFLA to chart a preservation course that will guide us through the rest of this century and into the next.

** *** ** *** **

The present text is a synopsis and analysis of preservation education opportunities. Thanks to my Vosper Fellowship, I was able to do research in this expanding field and to interview people from throughout the world who are involved in various aspects of preservation. Some of the following text emanates from information that I gleaned from the three slightly variant questionnaires that I distributed to educators, practitioners, and other people whose fields interact closely with preservation. (See Appendix B for the questionnaires.)

I have undertaken this study of preservation education in order to determine current and possible future directions of this field, and to make recommendations about ways in which IFLA might foster changes. I gathered my data not only through questionnaires, but also through interviews, informal discussions, and extensive research.

Fifty people representing eighteen countries were contacted; I interviewed personally and/or received questionnaires from 42 people representing 14 countries. The fifty were selected on the basis of their involvement in IFLA or their importance to the fields of conservation and preservation. (Seven people did not respond and one response was not usable.) The respondents' observations are interspersed throughout the book, wherever appropriate. Interviewees included 18 educators; 3 deans; 10 preservation administrators; 2 directors (library; regional conservation center); 2 preservation consultants; 3 researchers; 1 preservation journalist; and 3 representatives from granting agencies and foundations. Among the questions which I posed were three open-ended ones which were intended to stimulate creative ideas about the directions in which preservation education might go:

1) What do you see as the critical issues for the preservation field in the 1990s?

2) What steps should be taken to address these issues?

3) What are some international issues which the field must address?

By identifying emerging issues in the field at large, we can identify areas which need to be addressed in educational initiatives. Also, global trends will ultimately influence the structure into which educational programs will fit. In terms of course content, preservation curricula should not merely react to current activities but anticipate future ones. We must prepare students and practitioners to manage the increasingly complex resources at our disposal.

The responses to these questions resulted in numerous recommendations. These fell into seven broad areas: collaboration, educational activities, dissemination, resources, regional conservation treatment centers, research, and general strategies. These areas are summarized briefly below, and are also integrated into the chapters that follow.

A. Collaboration

Most interviewees expressed the concern that resources are shrinking and that that trend will not be reversed in the 1990s. Many felt that the short-term solution lies in creating more collaborative programs. Collaboration already exists in the United States among libraries of certain sizes or types (e.g., Association of Research Libraries, Research Libraries Group), but as one European interviewee put it, collaborative programs "must be pushed . . . even harder, and with a minimum of bureaucracy" to include all types of libraries and archives. There was concern expressed that programs organized through the European Community (EC) might get bogged down in red tape. Successful collaborations, on the other hand, will result in the cross-fertilization of ideas across library types, regions, and countries. As I will discuss in Chapter 3, several international organizations have already carried out successful collaborations and have laid the groundwork for new programs.

Collaborative projects will require STANDARDS, particularly in exchange formats, so we must continue to push for them.

B. Educational Activities

Although some of the educators I interviewed taught in venues other than library schools (e.g., the conservation programs in Italy), the library school faculty tended to be the most critical in their assessment of library school education. Although most British, French, German, Scandinavian, American, and Canadian library schools now offer at least one course in preservation, it is not usually integrated into the core courses, nor is it necessarily a required course. In the words of one American faculty member: "Library schools better get their act together." Her comment referred to the frequent use of adjunct rather than full-time faculty in the teaching of preservation, and the lack of preservation units in the core curricula.

Library schools, at least in the United States, are on *terra infirma.* The library profession must fight for the survival of its schools. Library school educators must be more responsive to the needs of the profession so that the profession will lobby aggressively for our survival. "Educational preparation of librarians will continue to be a priority concern throughout the 1990s, and frank conversations between library educators and practitioners about the nature of this education must take place now" (Dougherty and Hughes, *Preferred Futures*, 16). Yet, at the same time, preservationists must continue to view library schools as just one cog in the preservation education wheel, albeit a significant one. *Even if library schools do not survive, librarians, museum curators, and scholars, will still be responsible for preserving the human record. Conservation and preservation training will always be needed.*

Every library school has a different strength; preservation education initiatives can build on these. Some programs are strong in information science and could offer coursework in the preservation of electronic records; others are more traditionally based, and could focus on the preservation of paper-based records. For example, in the United States, the preservation and conservation programs at Columbia moved to the Graduate School of Library and Information Science at the University of Texas. Both of these library schools have had access to conservation laboratories. The School of Communication, Information and Library Studies at Rutgers offers a strong continuing education program with courses in preservation for practicing librarians and archivists. The students can take the courses towards a Professional Development Certificate in Preservation.

Recently, the library schools at Pittsburgh, UCLA, Texas, Wisconsin, and North Carolina collaborated in the design of the Preservation Intensive Institute (PII)--a week-long intensive comprising three seminars and offered in the summer. Drawing on individual library school strengths, the Institute will change locale each summer. The first PII was held at Pittsburgh in August 1993, and the next one will be held at UCLA in August 1994. (The first two Institutes received funding from the National Endowment for the Humanities.) The PII may lead to other collaborative preservation education efforts among library schools. The concept could work outside of the United States.

The interviewees had some broad recommendations for *all* library schools:

Broadly *educate* students; we now need to be "visionary not missionary." That is to say that we no longer need to convince people that preservation is important; now we must focus our efforts on responding to preservation issues in the virtual library.

Train part-time as well as full-time preservation administrators because a part-time administrator is better than no administrator at all. Also, with retrenchment in libraries, librarians tend more and more to have multiple responsibilities.

Increase educational outreach to the general public; they once needed to know about brittle paper and the proper storage and handling of books; now they also need to know about the newer formats such as videos and CDs.

Establish an international forum for those who teach preservation.

C. Dissemination of Preservation Information

The most frequent comment that was made during the course of the interviews was that although preservation information exists in abundance, it does not always get disseminated. A wide range of recommendations was made, including suggestions about the role that IFLA could play.

IFLA Recommendations

IFLA could do more to foster information exchange by:

- publishing the *International Preservation Newsletter* more often and more regularly;
- publishing a preservation column in the *IFLA Journal* in addition to the annual PAC report;
- building on the PAC Regional Centres to disseminate publications.

IFLA should also convene another international education conference like the one in Vienna in 1986; one should be convened every 10 years; so it is already time to plan for the next one.

General Recommendations

Establish a world-wide preservation network, perhaps on Internet, much like the Conservation Distribution List run out of Stanford University.

An international agency, like UNESCO, is also needed to disseminate information. Interviewees from all over the world complained, however, that it is extremely difficult to obtain the UNESCO Preservation Ramp Studies. So there was some doubt as to whether UNESCO is the best agency for dissemination.

The translation of publications to and from all languages is needed so that we can share information across borders. Right now, the Commission on Preservation and Access makes some of its publications available in Spanish, but texts need to be made available in more languages. A couple of interviewees recommended that IFLA look into machine translation; the technology is improving and even though the products are somewhat rough, at least more information would be available.

Editors of conservation and preservation journals should commission review articles of work being done in various parts of the world. *Conservation Administration News* currently runs such articles, but some interviewees would also like to see descriptions of preservation procedures and conservation techniques. These articles could be published in the *Abbey Newsletter, Conservation Administration News*, the *IFLA Journal, Restaurator,* the *International Preservation Newsletter*, or electronically, again, through the Internet.

Some interviewees felt that the dissemination of information is not enough; there must be feedback and an exchange of ideas. We can all learn from one another, and IFLA should try to promote the cross-fertilization of ideas. Also, countries with more developed preservation initiatives should mentor countries with less-developed ones, but we should continue to work towards south-to-south exchange programs (see Chapter 3). One interviewee who has consulted all over the world worried that some developing countries want to "jump on the technological bandwagon" when basic-level strategies are still needed. Finally, several interviewees indicated that we need more networking on an international level; clearly, this is already beginning to happen.

D. Resources and Funding

Preservation programs depend on a variety of resources including human, material, and monetary. All of these types can be shared across borders. Interviewees pointed out both the pros and cons of resource sharing. For example, a European respondent worried that the bureaucracy associated with European-Community-sponsored preservation committees might slow down the work. Another respondent, who works in the largest library in her country, lamented the inherently unequal relationships in their cooperative projects. Both agreed, however, that research sharing is important so that institutions do not replicate one another's work.

Preservation programs will continue to rely on outside funding sources as university and government resources shrink. Competition is keen for funds from granting agencies. A couple of interviewees recommended that more co-funding opportunities be explored, for example, between foundations and businesses. International companies involved in book distribution, deacidification, new technologies, etc. could be approached. Some American foundations are interested in funding initiatives in eastern Europe. There are numerous possibilities, but it will take some work to make them operative.

E. General Strategies

"The fortunes of preservation are closely tied with the fortunes of libraries. Preservation administrators must be part of the [overall library] solutions. Preservation will be placed on the back burner unless it stays in the forefront," observed one interviewee. Her solution? "In order for preservation and conservation specialists to play an active role, they must learn more about management." This can be accomplished through training programs as well as through continuing education courses.

Another interviewee stressed that libraries and archives must sustain current levels of preservation activity *even though* monetary resources are diminishing. (Other methods of support must be sought.) A certain amount of institutional commitment is needed, and preservation specialists must fight to make sure that those institutional resources are not withdrawn.

Other recommended strategies:

"Decide what action to take regarding the preservation of electronic media." *But* respond cautiously to technological developments; "we must not lose sight of the whole preservation picture."

Look to France and French work in image systems.

Work towards an international register of microform masters; the European Register of Microform Masters (EROMM) is a good start in that direction.

F. Regional Conservation Treatment Centers

The 1990s might be the right time to establish regional conservation centers throughout the world since cooperation is more prevalent than it used to be. In Europe, regional centers could be formed under the aegis of large cooperative efforts such as those sponsored by the EC. Recently, the Getty Conservation Institute announced that it will help set up a regional center in St. Petersburg, Russia. One interviewee felt that we should not necessarily view "regional" along country borders, but truly by regions.

G. Research

Several interviewees stressed the need for more conservation and preservation research. As one person put it, "We need to expand our definition of preservation to include information and the many physical manifestations thereof." Some of this research will take place in university settings, but by expanding the definition of preservation to include all physical manifestations of information, we have already begun to discover new venues for collaborative research with industry (see especially the research published by the Commission on Preservation and Access, some of which I will describe in Chapter 4).

The preservation prospects for this decade are both daunting and exciting. By the end of this century the educational landscape will be less sharply outlined as distance learning, computer-assisted instruction, and other technological innovations make the dissemination of information easier. IFLA can continue to play an important role in preservation education through its international network. We can look forward to these new initiatives.

** *** ** *** **

This text will consider all of the above delineated topics in greater detail in the following chapters. Chapter 2, "American Preservation Strategies," will examine the successes and failures of preservation education initiatives in the United States.

In chapter 3, "International Preservation Strategies," some international educational initiatives will be described. This chapter is not intended to be comprehensive; rather it will provide a sampling a various types of initiatives.

The preservation requirements for both book and nonbook formats and how our educational programs can respond to these needs is the topic of chapter 4, "The Preservation of Nonbook Formats: Implications for Education." The chapter also considers how conservation and preservation principles may need to be revised for the new forms of the book.

Chapter 5, "Resources for Preservation Education" considers the variety of resources — monetary, individual, and material — that we can draw on in developing educational programs.

The interdisciplinary nature of research in conservation and preservation is the topic of chapter 6, "Research and Development. The chapter also considers the implications of interdisciplinary research on educational programs.

Chapter 7, "The Dissemination of Information for Preservation Education" discusses ways in which preservation information can be more effectively distributed around the world. It considers both cooperative initiatives and new technologies that make dissemination easier.

Chapter 8, "What IFLA Can Do," provides a preservation education blueprint for the 1990s and offers specific recommendations to the IFLA PAC.

2. American Preservation Strategies

There are several organizations and activities that comprise American preservation strategies. Preservation education in the United States has been influenced by these strategies because many of the educators have also been preservation practitioners. Therefore, preservation practice has been a guiding force in the classroom.

Information about the preservation field must be gleaned from a variety of sources since a comprehensive history of American preservation has yet to be written. The first thorough look at any period of American preservation history was provided by Barbra Higginbotham in *Our Past Preserved: A History of American Library Preservation, 1876-1910* (Higginbotham). Perusing the annual reports of libraries, early American Library Association conference proceedings, and other contemporary sources, Higginbotham was able to chronicle preventive preservation measures that public and university librarians have practiced since the nineteenth century. The book established that preservation measures were being taken in numerous American libraries long before conservation and preservation were designated specialties within librarianship.

Perhaps the aspect of twentieth century preservation which is most distinctively American is the development of numerous professional and cooperative programs. Over the past 35 years, the work of these organizations has been crucial to the dissemination of preservation information. The development of some of these is discussed in Pamela W. Darling and Sherelyn Ogden's, "From Problems Perceived to Programs in Practice: The Preservation of Library Resources in the U.S.A., 1956-1980" (Darling/Ogden). They examine the role of such organizations as the Council on Library Resources and the Association of Research Libraries in the development of conservation and preservation, along with the development of early library programs.

The field of preservation administration has grown most substantially since 1974, when only a handful of libraries had preservation programs, most notably the Newberry Library, the Library of Congress, Yale, New York Public Library, and Columbia. From 1977 to 1991, 65 large academic libraries established programs which were run by administrators who devoted 50% or more of their time to preservation (Cloonan, *Organizing Preservation*, 8, fn. 1). Since 1984 ARL has compiled statistics on the growth and operation of individual programs (Association of Research Libraries, *ARL Preservation Statistics*).

The Andrew W. Mellon Foundation and Getty Trust, and agencies like the National Endowment for the Humanities and the National Historical Publications and Records Commission (NHPRC) have provided extensive funding for preservation activities in libraries and for the training of conservators and preservation administrators. NEH in particular has devoted a lot of resources to preservation. In 1985 the Office of Preservation was founded. Today it is the Division of Preservation and Access, the third largest grant-awarding section of NEH. Collectively, these funding agencies have fostered the growth of the preservation field as a whole in part because of the trickle-down effect. For example, over the past fifteen years, the Northeast Document Conservation Center (NEDCC) has received grants to do collection condition surveys in small libraries and historical societies. To date, NEDCC has surveyed several hundred institutions (Follow-up interview with Ann Russell, 10/6/93).

Yet the impact of external funding on the development of preservation in the United States has yet to be studied comprehensively. An article by John Hammer entitled "On the Political Aspects of Book Preservation in the U.S." describes the beginnings of federal support for preservation (22-40). And David Stam, on behalf of the Association of Research Libraries, the Commission on Preservation and Access, and the National Humanities Alliance, testified to the Committee on Appropriations of the U.S. House of Representatives in May 1993 concerning the significance of the preservation programs funded by NEH. But the purpose of his testimony was to insure future congressional funding for NEH, not to provide an in-depth analysis of the impact of such funding on the course of preservation activities in the United States (Stam).

The development of American preservation activities over the past fifteen years can be partially traced through the only two preservation periodicals published in the United States that are devoted solely the field: *The Abbey Newsletter: Bookbinding and Conservation* (1975-) and *Conservation Administration News* (1979-). *The Abbey Newsletter* was started by Ellen McCrady as the newsletter of the Academy Book Bindery in Dexter, Michigan. Originally it was sent to Academy Bindery ". . . customers, amateur and professional bookbinders, and friends" (*The Abbey Newsletter*, 1.3 [February 1976]: 1). As word of the *Newsletter* spread, its readership expanded; today there are about 1200 subscribers. After McCrady sold the Bindery she continued the *Newsletter* which has expanded in scope, size, and readership much as the field of preservation has.

Conservation Administration News (*CAN*), grew out of the Columbia Preservation Institute which was led by Paul Banks at Columbia University in the summer of 1978. In the words of Robert Patterson, the Editor, "*CAN* is a result of that . . . concern for preservation which the Columbia Institute nurtured. The inadequacy of formalized channels of communication about conservation was frequently discussed. As the last week of the gathering drew to its conclusion, . . . the idea of *CAN* was born. *CAN's* title was selected to stress . . . a positive approach to this often complex and frustrating subject" (Patterson, 3). Though *CAN* and *Abbey* are excellent publications, they cannot hope to cover all aspects of preservation and conservation comprehensively.

Since these periodicals were started in the 1970s, their titles include the term *conservation* rather than *preservation* (the evolution of the term *preservation* is discussed in chapter 1.) In the case of *Abbey* the term is still appropriate since McCrady focuses heavily on conservation. For *CAN*, which is more administrative in scope, *Preservation Administration News* would perhaps be more appropriate, but unfortunately its acronym would then become *PAN*, which is not necessarily what the editors wished to convey.

That Americans have tended to take cooperative and consortial approaches to preservation problems is well illustrated by the founding of *CAN*: several librarians at the Columbia Preservation Institute were responsible for its creation. Americans have also organized activities through professional organizations such as the American Library Association (ALA), the Council on Library Resources, the American Institute for Conservation of Historic and Artistic Works (AIC), the Association of Research Libraries, the Research Libraries Group (RLG), the Society of American Archivists (SAA), and, more recently, the Commission on Preservation and Access.

The American Library Association

As early as 1908, the American Library Association had a Committee on Bookbinding, but it was not until 1923 that it became a standing committee (Stratton, 303). From the 1920s through 1950s the Committee focused on library binding issues. Gradually, as interest in other aspects of preservation—such as permanent-durable paper—grew the Bookbinding Committee became the Committee on Preservation of Library Materials. Finally, in 1979 the Committee received section status and it became the Preservation of Library Materials Section within the Resources and Technical Services Division (Darling/Ogden, 23), now the Association for Library Collections & Technical Services (ALCTS). Since 1980, PLMS and the closely related Reproduction of Library Materials Section (RLMS) have sponsored numerous ALA programs and institutes, and have published manuals and directories. ALCTS is currently restructuring itself; PLMS and RLMS may merge into one section.

In 1989 the then ALA President Patricia Wilson Berger appointed the President's Committee on Preservation Policy. Forming the Committee was in keeping with Berger's focus on literacy, preservation, and access to information. The Committee was charged with writing a policy which outlined the responsibilities of the library profession as a whole in preserving library collections regardless of format. The Committee wrote drafts and submitted them for review to all ALA divisions. The final draft was approved by the ALA Council, and appears in the *ALA Handbook, 1992-93* in section 52.2, *Services and Responsibilities of Libraries. Preservation.* Here is an excerpt:

> The American Library Association, with its history of concern and action in the preservation of information resources, affirms that such preservation is central to libraries and librarianship. In particular, ALA affirms that the preservation of library resources is essential to protect the public's right to the free flow of information as embodied in the First Amendment to the Constitution and the Library Bill of Rights.
>
> The Association's preservation concerns are not limited to information recorded on paper but include information disseminated on other media such as film, magnetic tape, and digital disks. ALA believes that manufacturers, publishers and purchasers of information in any medium must address the usability, durability and longevity of resources published and disseminated in both electronic and traditional formats. . . .
>
> The American Library Association . . . will work closely with standards-setting organizations to identify and develop needed preservation standards and to promote compliance. (145)

If this policy is practiced, it has the potential to become an effective lobbying tool for librarians when they negotiate with grant agencies, publishers, and other information providers.

The Council on Library Resources

CLR, founded in 1956 with money from the Ford Foundation, has always promoted research in preservation and conservation. Its first director, Verner Clapp, supported William Barrow's research into the causes of deterioration in paper. Later, when Barrow was working on the manufacture of permanent book paper, CLR continued to back him. (The remarkable relationship between Barrow and Clapp is chronicled in William J. Crowe's dissertation, "Verner W. Clapp As Opinion Leader and Change Agent in the Preservation of Library Materials.") After Clapp's retirement, CLR also provided Richard D. Smith with partial funding for the Wei T'o nonaqueous deacidification process (Crowe, 102-103).

During his tenure at CLR, Clapp also helped to establish the Library Technology Program of the American Library Association. LTP has sponsored research into the various materials and equipment that librarians use. Much of the research has culminated in publications. Two of LTP's early projects were on the longevity of the Se-Lin system for call number labels, and the development of standards for permanent/durable catalog cards. Four preservation-related publications are also of note: Carolyn Horton's *Cleaning and Preserving Bindings and Related Materials* (1967 & 1969); Bernard Middleton's *The Restoration of Leather Bindings* (1972); and George Martin Cunha's "Mass Deacidification in Libraries" (1987) and "Mass Deacidification in Libraries: 1989 Update."

By the end of the 1970s, CLR began to rely more heavily on the committee approach for tackling preservation issues. Committee membership included library leaders, university administrators, and representatives from scholarly associations. One of these committees led to the formation of the Commission on Preservation and Access which has also followed CLR's committee model.

The Commission on Preservation and Access

In 1986, CLR established the Committee on Preservation and Access to examine national preservation initiatives and to promote the interests of the national library and archival community. (The Commission has always approached preservation as a federal concern, though in recent years it has initiated international projects as well; see Chapter 3). In 1988, the Commission became an independent, non-profit organization. Brittle books was established as its first priority. It has sponsored research (continuing, and in fact taking over, CLR's preservation activities), organized task forces, presented institutes, and published many technical reports. The Commission is supported by university and corporate sponsorships and by grants.

Of particular interest to the International Federation of Library Associations, is that the Commission, more than any other American organization except the Getty Conservation Institute, has become involved in numerous international preservation activities, particularly in the area of reformatting. The Review and Assessment Committee which evaluated the Commission in 1991 recommended that the International Project be continued and enlarged (recommendation #6, 24 of their *Final Report*)--perhaps from the realization that no single country can solve all preservation problems.

The only director of CPA has been Patricia Battin, who will retire in 1994. She has set the tone and agenda for the Commission. The 1991 Review and Assessment Committee *Final Report*, noted that some people felt that the Commission has been overly concerned with brittle books and reformatting to the exclusion of preserving original documents (18). Other commentators felt that "the Commission should focus its resources on the development of a national strategy for preservation" (19). The Review and Assessment Committee recommended that the Commission develop a strategy for the preservation of rare books (recommendation #12, 28) and that the Board of Directors consider a "National Preservation Management Strategy" (recommendation #16, 31).

The Review and Assessment Committee also recommended that the Commission maintain the practice of quinquennial review (recommendation #3, 22); if it does so, the Commission will surely continue to reassess its programs. A reassessment on a regular schedule is necessary in a field which changes as rapidly as does this one, with its continuing dialogue and close association with scientists and practitioners throughout the world.

American Institute for Conservation of Historic and Artistic Works

AIC originated in the 1950s as the International Institute for Conservation—American Group (IIC-AG). In 1972 AIC was incorporated as a non-profit organization, ". . . for persons engaged in the conservation and restoration of historic and artistic works in order that they may exchange . . . and advance knowledge and improved methods of art conservation and restoration" (*Articles of Incorporation, 1972, AIC Directory, 1994,* 10.)

In 1979 six Specialty Groups were established, one of which was the Book and Paper Group (BPG). Many librarians and book conservators belong to BPG, which publishes *The Book and Paper Annual*, a compilation of information on current conservation practices. Volume 11 of this successful annual appeared in 1992. Joint initiatives between ALA and AIC are coordinated through formal liaisons.

Association of Research Libraries

Verner Clapp worked with ARL in order to promote preservation initiatives. In 1960, ARL appointed a standing Committee on Preservation in response to William Barrow's CLR-sponsored work on the manufacture of permanent and durable paper (Crowe, 82). Clapp collaborated closely with the Committee, attending many of its meetings (Crowe, 83). After Clapp's death in 1972, the ARL Committee articulated plans for new cooperative approaches to preservation. Among ARL's preservation initiatives have been: 1) *Spec Kits*—booklets on all aspects of academic librarianship which contain procedural information submitted by cooperating libraries; several have focused on preservation procedures (e.g. #66 *Planning for Preservation*, #70 *Basic Preservation Procedures*, and #160 *Preservation Organization and Staffing*); 2) the Preservation Planning Program which comprises both a consultancy service and publications; and 3) the publication of annual preservation statistics which have now been gathered for nearly a decade.

The most comprehensive of the ARL preservation initiatives is the Preservation Planning Program which was first designed in 1979 with NEH funding. The purpose of the program is to develop a self-study procedure so that libraries can identify and address their preservation problems (*Preservation Planning Program: An Assisted Self-Study Manual for Libraries*, 1987, i). The first *Manual* was published in 1982; it was revised and expanded in 1987. In 1993, the *Manual* was supplemented by seven Preservation Planning Program resource guides which cover such topics as the replacement and reformatting of library materials, library binding, collections conservation, and disaster preparedness.

Research Libraries Group

The Research Libraries Group started out as a consortium of Harvard, Yale, Columbia, and the New York Public Library; it was incorporated in 1974. In 1980 RLG moved to Palo Alto, California. Its mission was and still is "to improve access to information needed for education and scholarship" (McClung, 61). Four core areas were developed in order in order to accomplish this: "cooperative bibliographic control of information and materials for research; effective mechanisms for sharing information and materials among participating institutions; expanded and coordinated collection development efforts; and preservation of the collections, either in original or surrogate formats" (McClung, 61).

Perhaps best known for the development of the national bibliographic database RLIN, RLG has also organized committees which address issues of concern for research libraries. It has had a preservation committee since 1975, though it was later reorganized in 1980 (McClung, 62-63) as RLG expanded to include more members. Most influential of the committee's projects has been the development of national preservation microfilming standards which culminated in the revised 1987 publication *Preservation Microfilming: A Guide for Librarians and Archivists* (Nancy E. Gwinn, ed.). This work was recently revised again by RLG's Nancy Elkington under the title, *RLG Preservation Microfilming Handbook* (Elkington).

RLG has managed several successful cooperative microfilming projects focusing on the so-called "great-collections" of books and archives in RLG-member libraries. The projects began in 1983 with funding by NEH. According to a recent ARL report, from 1986-1992, RLG received $5,745,754 from NEH in preservation microfilming grants (*Report of. . . the Review of the NEH Preservation Program*, Appendix 3).

RLG has used RLIN to support preservation programs. For example, in the course of developing cooperative microfilming projects a feature known as "queuing" was added to the system. Queuing is a system for libraries to input short bibliographic records into RLIN. These records let other libraries know that a given title is being microfilmed thereby helping to decrease the chances that libraries will duplicate filming efforts. RLG also designed the first online catalog of master microform masters.

Other Programs

Other organizations have run important preservation programs, including the Society of American Archivists, SOLINET, and AMIGOS. Additionally, regional conservation centers have offered courses, workshops, conservation surveys, disaster recovery assistance, and so on. One regional center, the Northeast Document Conservation Center in Andover, Massachusetts, celebrated its twentieth anniversary in 1993.

A National Preservation Program

In 1962, the ARL Committee on Preservation commissioned Gordon Williams, Director of the Center for Research Libraries, to develop a national plan for preservation (Crowe, 83). The resulting report, underwritten by CLR, was completed in 1964 (Williams). Although the report spelled out recommendations, Clapp felt that it did not constitute a plan (Crowe, 84). In 1965, ARL (and Clapp) recommended that the Library of Congress implement a national preservation program (Darling/Ogden, 12). LC was already engaged in CLR-funded projects. One of these was the 1965 publication of the first volumes of the *National Register of Microform Masters*.

In 1965 LC agreed to develop a national program. In 1967, Frazer Poole, who had previously worked for the Library Technology Program, became LC's first Preservation Officer. At around the same period, Norman Shaffer directed the CLR-funded Pilot Preservation Project (Darling/Ogden, 13), which dealt with the brittle-books problem. The preservation department grew steadily and a conservation treatment laboratory was set up. Peter Waters, who had spent time in Florence organizing salvage efforts after the flood of November 1966, joined the LC staff. (His *Salvage of Water-Damaged Materials,* first published in 1975, was distributed without charge.) In 1973 the recently established Preservation Research and Testing Office began working on the development of Diethyl Zinc (DEZ) mass deacidification (Cloonan, "Mass Deacidification," 97), some of this research was also funded by CLR.

In the 1970s and 1980s, the Library of Congress published a series of preservation leaflets. These dealt with such topics as preserving newspapers. *National Preservation News,* an occasional newsletter, began publication in 1985. LC also established a preservation reference service. From 1986-1991, under the direction of Merrily Smith, LC was the international focal point for the International Federation of Library Associations (IFLA) Preservation and Conservation Core Programme.

However, deep budget cuts coupled with the expense and problems related to the DEZ project at LC has diminished the size and importance of its national preservation efforts in recent years. With NEH supporting national efforts such as the U.S. Newspaper Program and the brittle books program; with so many professional organizations offering preservation services; and with the Commission on Preservation and Access focusing on national issues, it now seems unlikely that LC will ever expand its national preservation program again to the level that it was from the late 1960s through the early 1980s.

Other National Initiatives

The American preservation community has sought to establish national preservation policies as well as programs. CPA and ARL worked with key congressional members to develop a permanent paper policy which eventually became the *Joint Resolution To establish a national policy on permanent paper*. The process that led to the introduction of this legislation is described by Hammer (32-38). It passed both the House and the Senate, and was signed into law by President George Bush on October 12, 1990 (Public Law 101-423). The resolution states that,

> Section 1. It is the policy of the United States that Federal records, books and publications of enduring value be produced on acid free permanent papers.
>
> Section 2. The Congress of the United States urgently recommends that—
>
> (1) Federal agencies require the use of acid free permanent paper for publications of enduring value produced by the Government Printing Office or produced by Federal grant or contract, using the specifications for such paper established by the Joint Committee on Printing;
>
> (2) Federal agencies require the use of archival quality acid free papers for permanently valuable Federal records and confer with National Archives and Records Administration on the requirements for paper quality;
>
> (3) American publishers and State and local governments use acid free papers for publications of enduring value in voluntary compliance with the American National Standard;
>
> (4) all publishers, private and governmental, prominently note the use of acid free permanent paper in books, advertisements, catalogs, and standard bibliographic listings;
> and
>
> (5) the Secretary of State, Librarian of Congress, Archivist of the United States . . . make known the national policy regarding acid free permanent papers to foreign governments . . . since the acid paper problem is worldwide and essential foreign materials being imported by our libraries are printed on acid papers.
>
> Section 3. The Librarian of Congress, the Archivist of the United States, and the Public Printer shall jointly monitor the Federal Government's progress in implementing the national policy . . . .

The White House Conference on Library and Information Services (WHCLIS) is another national forum for setting library policy. The Conference, first held in 1979, will take place every twelve years, providing a forum at which delegates from all over the United States and its territories can address library issues. The President of the United States writes a summary report of the conference which is then submitted to Congress. Recommendations made at WHCLIS can be taken back to individual states, where grass root work on implementation begins. "Whether the specific recommendations ever become law is less important than the fact that WHCLIS has given birth to the citizen movement for libraries that began in 1979 . . ." (Berry/Quinn, 46). At the 1991 White House Conference on Library and Information Services, one of the 94 policy recommendations was for a formal national preservation policy (Berry/Quinn, 46). President Bush's report to Congress stated that, "From colonial times forward, our libraries have acquired, preserved, and disseminated information to Americans" (*Library Journal*, 117.7 (April 15, 1992): 15). Bush's use of the term *preserved* implies a historical action. Yet most librarians use the term *preserva*tion in a pro-active way. We must make a national commitment to preserve information in all formats. It is now up to the library community to promote these preservation policy initiatives.

The ALA Preservation Policy, the National Policy on Permanent Paper, and the WHCLIS are three examples of policy initiatives that have helped to instill a public awareness of preservation. Higginbotham describes the ALA Preservation Policy as emphasizing "the fundamental importance of a public conscience as the path to legislation and funding" (Higginbotham/Jackson, x).

* * *

At the beginning of this chapter I pointed out that the United States is distinctive from other countries in the number and variety of its cooperative preservation initiatives. There are over a hundred major research libraries many of which have their own preservation programs. Many of these same libraries, and scores of smaller ones, participate in cooperative preservation projects. This pluralism may explain the failure of the Library of Congress to sustain a national preservation program. Since other national organizations have had long-standing commitments to the field, and since resources shrunk at LC while increasing elsewhere, it is not surprising that LC is no longer the center of national preservation efforts. Further, although LC is not a national library it *is* a federal library, which makes it ineligible to receive grants from other federal agencies such as NEH. The decentralized approach to national preservation problem-solving is likely to continue, and there will probably never be only one national preservation program in the United States. Rather, we are likely to see the push for more national policies.

Preservation Strategies and Education

The strategies I have discussed provide the groundwork for understanding American approaches to preservation education. There are two fundamental characteristics of American education: most of the educators have been practitioners, so that the approach has been more practical than theoretical, and educational opportunities have been provided by nearly all of the organizations described above as well as by library schools. Further, many educational opportunities have also been cooperative. For example, the American Library Association has offered library binding courses in conjunction with the Library Binding Institute, and the Preservation Intensive Institute (PII) was designed cooperatively by the preservation faculty at the University of Pittsburgh, the University of California at Los Angeles, the University of Wisconsin at Madison, the University of Texas, and the University of North Carolina at Chapel Hill.

Paul N. Banks taught the first library school course devoted exclusively to the preservation of library materials at the University of Illinois in 1971; the second such course was taught by George M. Cunha at the University of Rhode Island in 1974, as I mentioned in Chapter 1. These men were practitioners: Banks started the preservation program at the Newberry Library and Cunha founded the Northeast Document Conservation Center. Cunha and Banks have no academic degrees in conservation; both, in fact, were partially self-taught. That is how the pattern of practitioners as teachers began. After Banks and Cunha, the next group of preservation educators was also made up of practitioners. This group included Pamela Darling, Sally Buchanan, Merrily Smith, Sherelyn Ogden, Ann Russell, Michèle Cloonan, Carolyn Harris, Susan Swartzburg and Gay Walker.

Three other models developed: 1) a few full-time library school faculty began to study preservation and integrate it into their courses. Judith Serebnick (Indiana University) integrated preservation into her collection management courses, and Lois Upham (University of South Carolina) included preservation units in her technical services course (Cloonan, "Preservation Education, 192-194). 2) Gerald Lundeen (University of Hawaii), a scientist who became a library school educator, taught a preservation course with an emphasis on causes of paper deterioration. He also edited the Fall 1981 *Conservation of Library Materials* issue for *Library Trends* (30.2). 3) Josephine Fang (Simmons College) developed a team-teaching approach with Sherelyn Ogden and Ann Russell of NEDCC. This course on conservation and preservation of library materials has been in the Simmons curriculum since 1981. Fang has also been active in promoting preservation education internationally; she was one of the organizers of the 1986 IFLA/Vienna conference, "Preservation of Library Materials" (edited by Fang/Russell; interview with Fang, 7/2/93). John DePew has taught a preservation course for a number of years at Florida State University, and he wrote the first preservation textbook (DePew).

How has the predominantly practical approach to preservation affected preservation education? The most visible affect has been the paucity of theoretical research. The theoretical work has generally been in the realm of conservation science and has dealt primarily with the deterioration of library materials and deacidification. More recently there has been research in the areas of nonbook formats, but the point is that little preservation-related research is being undertaken by faculty in schools of library and information science. The two doctoral dissertations cited in this chapter (Higginbotham, Columbia University and Crowe, Indiana University) were written under the direction of library historians *not preservationists*. While it is good that library historians recognize the importance of preservation, preservation educators should also be promoting doctoral research.

Since schools of library and information science exist in university settings where the commitment to research is high, one might question whether preservation education belongs in library schools. If preservation *does* belong in graduate education, then research should be fostered there. We must look at preservation education with a critical eye: if it is truly only practical, then it can be carried out as well by professional associations such as ALA and ARL as it can by schools of library science. But if we believe that preservation has theoretical underpinnings as well, then we must promote a more rigorous research agenda. By looking more closely at the nature of research in our field, we can determine the best domain for preservation education.

As discussed in chapter 1, library schools in the United States have been closed in many universities. One rationale for closure is that the research emerging from these schools is not rigorous enough. Also, library schools are seen as promoting the practical rather than the theoretical. But such rationales are suspicious; small professional schools such as social work and nursing are also being closed while large and wealthy professional schools such as law and business are thriving. What university administrators do not want to admit in public forums is that small professional schools do not generate much revenue.

Given the uncertain status of many library schools, it is perhaps all the more important for us to evaluate whether or not these schools are the best settings for preservation education. But first we need to evaluate the theoretical fit: assuming that library schools are secure, are they the best places for preservation education? And what is the role of preservation research?

In chapter 6 I will consider the role of research and development in preservation, and in the final chapter I will offer suggestions about how IFLA can promote international research initiatives.

3. International Preservation Strategies

Clinton urged the major U.S. trading partners to take specific measures to promote economic growth, and he called for cooperation among all countries to coordinate trade policies. . . .

Clinton asserted, 'We simply cannot afford to work at cross purposes with the other major industrial democracies. Our major partners must work harder and more closely with us to reduce interest rates, stimulate investment, reduce structural barriers to trade and restore robust global growth. (*Facts on File*, March 4, 1993, p. 140.)

The European Commission May 12 approved the conclusions of a report that expressed the EC's support for NAFTA [North American Free Trade Agreement]. The study saw mostly positive benefits for Mexico, and for the EC's relationship with that country. The report also listed certain areas of trade—including agriculture, financial services and service industries in general—where EC businesses might be harmed, noting that the EC would seek to negotiate tariff reductions to minimize the anticipated negative effect. (*Facts on File*, May 20, 1993, p. 363.)

The United Nations General Assembly Sept. 21 opened its 48th session . . . at its headquarters in New York City. Speakers from several countries, including U.S. President Clinton, addressed the body . . . .

In his most comprehensive foreign policy address [yet], . . . U.S. President Clinton Sept. 27 aimed to demonstrate his commitment to an active U.S. foreign policy, and urged the expansion of market democracies. (*Facts on File*, September 30, 1993, p. 719.)

The European Community's Treaty on European Union went into effect Nov. 1. The so-called Maastricht Treaty went into force nearly two years after EC leaders had agreed to the pact at a December 1991 summit in Maastricht, the Netherlands.

The treaty's provisions sought to create 'an ever-closer union among the peoples of Europe.'

The pact created a new 12-nation 'European Union,' and citizens of the 12 nations acquired several new rights. These included the right to petition the European Parliament and the right to file complaints with an ombudsman appointed by the parliament.

The treaty also

> Set a goal of 1999 for the creation of a single European currency . . . . (*Facts on File,* November 4, 1993, p. 831.)

The implementation of the European Community's Treaty on European Union (also known as the Maastricht Treaty) and the passage of the North American Free Trade Agreement in the U.S. Congress—both in 1993—demonstrate the international movement towards economic cooperation. Illustrating this mood, Anthony Lake, President Clinton's national security advisor, recently outlined current U.S. foreign-policy goals: "enlargement of the world's free community of market democracies" will replace the concept of the containment of communism as the central focus of U.S. policy (*Facts on File,* October 28, 1993, p. 804). Though both NAFTA and the Maastricht Treaty are also concerned with issues of immigration, the environment, and foreign and security policy, enhancing economic relationships seemed to be the primary driving force in 1993. Today, countries' economies are so interdependent that August 1993 saw a near collapse of the present exchange rate mechanism of the European Monetary System.

It is too soon to tell what effects these political unions will have on the future of international preservation education initiatives. Certainly within the 12-country EC, continuing education and internship opportunities could develop more easily now that the Treaty on European Union has designated the goals of "developing the European dimension in education . . . encouraging mobility of students and teachers . . . [and] promoting cooperation between educational establishments" (quoted in Peter Vodosek, "The Internationalization of Information," p. 314).

In the meantime, only a handful of countries are linked by the Treaty on European Union and NAFTA. Opportunities for other countries will necessarily be different. For example, work and internship opportunities can be organized through channels such as IFLA which currently supports internships through its network of Regional Centres (e.g., the National Diet Library in Tokyo recently trained a restorer from the Malaysian National Archives. See Jean-Marie Arnoult, "Annual Report 1991-92," 214). Possible future directions can be charted from existing programs.

** *** ** *** **

A look at current international preservation strategies must necessarily be kaleidoscopic, for there is in the world a constantly changing set of circumstances, players, and political, economic, and social events. This chapter will examine some cooperative international programs as well as a few individual programs (Table B).

No single country can solve all conservation and preservation problems, but each can contribute something that will add to the longevity of the world's cultural heritage. Technologically rich countries like France, the UK, Germany, Canada, and the U.S. conduct research on the deacidification of paper, paper strengthening, and the longevity of non-book formats. Countries that are less technologically advanced may have strong traditions of craftsmanship and therefore individuals who can be trained to undertake newly-developed conservation treatments. Also, poorer countries must necessarily take a more pragmatic approach--they may find ingenious low-tech solutions to caring for individual items or collections. A look at some educational initiatives around the world will illustrate these various approaches.

The Cooperative Tradition

Ideally, cooperation diminishes the duplication of efforts among countries and organizations. When duplication is avoided, it is sometimes also possible to reduce the expenditure of funds and other resources. Cooperative projects may be labor intensive in the beginning stages, yet the labor expended at the outset may save time in the long run. Three of the organizations described below, IFLA, UNESCO, and ICA, have been working together since the 1970s. They have demonstrated that effective strategies for cooperative approaches to the needs of information professionals can be implemented.

A united effort to coordinate preservation and conservation education programs must necessarily pose obstacles because the needs of and resources in individual countries are inevitably quite different. For example, library school education exists at both the undergraduate and graduate levels. Although in the United States a master's degree is required for professional work, in many other countries the undergraduate degree is all that is required. Even at the master's degree level there are great differences. In the United States alone there are nine-month, twelve-month, and twenty-four month programs. Yet each of these programs leads to an accredited master's degree. So any international educational program designed for library students or professional librarians must be planned with these disparities in mind.

The programs described below have tackled these problems in various ways. IFLA has issued recommendations for preservation *content* in library schools (see Feather, *Guidelines,* below) and has not focused on the overall structural differences of library school programs. UNESCO has supported only the first—the master's in library science—graduate degree, designing curricula to fit the twenty-four month program (Large, "Curriculum Development," 79, and see below).

IFLA

IFLA has long been interested in the preservation of the world's cultural heritage. Through standing committees within IFLA and joint projects with UNESCO and the International Council on Archives, IFLA has offered many educational opportunities throughout the world. Recognizing the growing importance of preservation and conservation in libraries worldwide, in 1984 IFLA established the Preservation and Conservation (PAC) Core Programme. The PAC was launched in 1986 at the IFLA-sponsored Vienna Conference, a significant international gathering of conservators, preservation administrators, and educators (Merrily A. Smith, ed., *Preservation of*

Library Materials). Through 1991, the PAC International Focal Point was the Library of Congress in Washington; in 1992 it moved to the Bibliothèque Nationale in Paris.

The *IFLA Annual Reports* for 1987-1991 document the range of activities for both the PAC and the Conservation Section. These include the development of guidelines for teaching preservation in library schools (Feather, *Guidelines*, and discussed further, below); a UNESCO-funded review of training needs in preservation and conservation; participation in the European Register of Microform Masters (EROMM); sponsorship of seminars throughout the world; and initiating national and international programs of work in cooperation with PAC through the development Regional Centres (*IFLA Annual Reports, 1988-1991*). These Centres are located at the Library of Congress (Washington, D.C.), Deutsche Bibliothek (Leipzig), Biblioteca Nacional (Caracas), National Library of Australia (Canberra), and National Diet Library in Tokyo (Arnoult, "Annual Report 1991-92").

John Feather's *Guidelines for the Teaching of Preservation to Librarians, Archivists, and Documentalists for a Joint Working Party of IFLA's Sections on Conservation and Education and Training,* stemmed from IFLA's commitment to training and education. The goal of the *Guidelines* was to help librarians solve conservation and preservation problems within the context of library management (Feather, 2). Feather suggested three levels of educational programs: Basic, Intermediate, and Specialist. The Basic level of conservation and preservation awareness should be included in general core library school courses since "all information professionals are dependent upon the physical integrity of the information resource, whether it is a manuscript or a floppy disk" (7). Courses which should address preservation issues include library management, technical services, collection management, and serials. Intermediate-level students (those whose careers might be in middle or senior management posts) would take several courses in areas which include preservation components, as well as a preservation course, if offered. The specialist level is for those who will pursue careers as archivists or rare book librarians. This course of study would be more comprehensive still.

The *Guidelines* do not specify a course of study for students who want to become preservation administrators. In the United States, several library schools offer a preservation specialization (e.g. Pittsburgh, Rutgers, Texas, and UCLA). These programs combine coursework with independent studies, internships, and sometimes specialization papers. In Chapter 7, the possibility for distance learning programs in preservation will be discussed. Such programs would make it possible for students from countries with few preservation course offerings to supplement their educational opportunities. In Chapter 8, IFLA's potential role in stimulating such programs will be considered.

IFLA's network of conservation and preservation programs through the PAC Regional Centres is continuing to expand. With such an infrastructure in place, there are plenty of opportunities for developing new educational initiatives at the regional level.

UNESCO

The United Nations Educational, Scientific, and Cultural Organization, (UNESCO) was founded in 1945. From the beginning UNESCO has been interested in establishing programs of library and information services, particularly in developing countries (Large, 77). UNESCO has demonstrated a commitment to developing a professional library-and-archives work force because of shortages of such personnel in many parts of the world. Fellowships, scholarships, travel grants, international courses and seminars, teacher exchanges, and the establishment of new library schools have all been supported by UNESCO (Large, 77-78).

UNESCO has worked with IFLA, the International Federation for Information and Documentation (FID), and the International Council on Archives (ICA) to coordinate the education of librarians, information scientists, and archivists. As I mentioned above, UNESCO has supported IFLA projects such as its study of preservation and conservation training needs.

F. Wilfrid Lancaster has reviewed the education activities of UNESCO from the perspective of one who has taught in its programs since 1974 ("What has UNESCO Achieved in Education and Training for the Information Professions?"). Preservation and conservation courses have long been included in the offerings. UNESCO has sought to achieve "a maximum multiplier effect"; that is, courses have been offered to educators and potential educators, the assumption being that some of them would return to their own countries and disseminate what they learned in the classroom. To date, it is impossible to determine if this has been achieved since no study has yet been undertaken to measure the results of this educational method. Similarly, it is not possible to know whether the "potential educators" actually became educators.

Lancaster feels that the quality of students in UNESCO-sponsored courses has been uneven. Although participants are supposed to have some background in the subject areas in which they are taking classes, some participants have had none at all. Lancaster thinks that this may be because some governments promote the candidacy of well connected rather than well qualified candidates.

One problem with international courses stems from cultural diversity issues. Lancaster describes a course which brought together participants from Latin America, the Caribbean, Africa, Asia, Poland, and the Soviet Union. "The frame of reference of a participant from, say, Uganda is likely to be quite different from that of one from Poland, and what they need to gain from a course might be quite different too" (72). This problem is not unique to UNESCO; it would exist for any course with such a diverse student body. UNESCO has addressed the issue by offering more regional courses (72).

An inevitable weakness with international programs stems from what is referred to as North-to-South exchange—the relationship between developed and less-developed countries. Most UNESCO training programs have involved teachers from developed countries and students from less-developed countries. UNESCO is exploring more South-to-South exchange programs. In a 1991 issue of the *UNISIST* (United Nations Intergovernment System of Information in Science and Technology) *Newsletter* is a description of four post-graduate programs in information science: one in Venezuela, one in China, and two in Africa (Nigeria and Ethiopia). ". . . [T]here are now in many developing countries dedicated experts who are capable of identifying needs, setting objectives, designing projects, securing and managing resources and finally implementing successful programmes where the co-operation between multilateral and bilateral agencies, on the one hand, and national authorities, on the other, is on an equal footing. This new approach indicates that the assistance which has been provided in the past is now bearing fruit, as local expertise now exists on site and complementary resources are only needed to reach impressive results" ("Post-Graduate Programmes in Information Science," 51). As the core of experts expands in these less-developed countries, South-to-South initiatives should follow.

UNESCO has also made significant contributions to conservation and preservation education through its publications. One notable series has been sponsored by UNESCO, the General Information Program and UNISIST. Known as the *UNESCO RAMP Studies*, (RAMP = Records and Archives Management Programme), the series has covered such topics as disaster recovery, the preservation of library materials in the tropics, the impact of environmental pollution on preservation, and Y. P. Kathpalia's guidelines for training preservation specialists (*A Model Curriculum for the Training of Specialists in Document Preservation and Restoration*--see also Table D). These free publications are provided upon written request to UNESCO's headquarters in Paris. However, several interviewees complained that these useful publications are very difficult to obtain; UNESCO does not always respond to written requests, and sometimes the wrong studies are mailed out. (In the United States, the West Virginia Library Commission will lend them on microfiche or provide paper copies for a fee [telephone call to Karen Goff at the West Virginia Library Commission, February 23, 1993]).

UNESCO has recently initiated a world-wide "Memory of the World" project which has a comprehensive preservation component. One aspect of the initiative will be to explore all of the ramifications of new technologies on preservation of the written record. The project was described at the 1993 IFLA Conference held in Barcelona.

ICA

The International Council on Archives was founded in 1948 and definitively established in 1950 at the lst International Congress of Archives at Paris (*Yearbook of International Organizations, 1992/93*). Its aims are to promote the preservation and use of archives through research, professional training, and the dissemination of professional standards throughout the world. ICA is organized into five sections, one of which is the Section for Archival Education and Training (ICA/SAE). There are also about a dozen committees and working groups including the Conservation and Restoration Committee (ICA/CCR).

ICA has contributed to the RAMP studies, and has participated with both IFLA and UNESCO on joint projects. One of these, *Preservation and Conservation of Library Documents: A UNESCO/IFLA/ICA Enquiry into the Current State of the World's Patrimony*, was published as a RAMP Study in 1987. The "International Programme of Microfilming," which films archival materials in developing countries, is an ICA and UNESCO project. The ICA publishes a "Handbooks Series" with K. G. Saur; some of these publications deal with the preservation and conservation of archives.

Further educational collaboration with the ICA should be explored. Perhaps regional training opportunities could be coordinated between the nine ICA regional branches and the IFLA/PAC Regional Centres.

The Commission on Preservation and Access

The establishment and structure of the Commission was described in Chapter 2; some of the research projects which it has funded will be described in Chapter 4. The significant feature of the Commission for the present discussion is its International Program.

This Program, also called the International Project, was begun in 1988 "to explore the feasibility of creating an international database of records for preserved materials" (Hans Rütimann, *The International Project [Progress Report]*, 1). Since then, it has expanded to include other initiatives, mostly in the area of preservation microfilming For example, it participates in the European Register of Microform Masters (EROMM). As of August 1992, it was involved in microfilming projects in Algeria, Australia, Austria, Brazil, Brunei, Canada, Chile, China, Denmark, Egypt, Finland, France, Germany, Great Britain, Hungary, Ireland, Israel, Japan, Liechtenstein, Philippines, Poland, Singapore, South Africa, Spain, Sweden, Switzerland, Syria, Taiwan, Tunisia, and Venezuela (Rütimann, *The International Project 1992 Update*). Much of this work was funded by the Mellon Foundation.

UNESCO has asked the Commission to take part in the planning of the "Memory of the World" project described above (The Commission on Preservation and Access, *Annual Report, July 1 1992-June 30, 1993*, 9). Such a collaboration may lead to new directions for the Commission.

A June 1993 Commission-sponsored meeting of international scholars in Bellagio, Italy led to the recommendation by the participants to establish a European Commission on Preservation and Access. The start-up will be supported by the International Project (*Annual Report, July 1, 1992-June 30, 1993*, 11)

In the area of education, most of the Commission's work has been with American programs, though it did provide funding for the MicrogrAphic Preservation Services (MAPS) to sponsor 11-week internships for three staff members from Die Deutsche Bibliothek in Leipzig. It also funded two librarians from Central American countries to attend a seminar in the United States (*Annual Report, July 1, 1992-June 30, 1993, 10-11).*

The International Project might look into further educational initiatives outside of the United States, particularly in the area of internships which it could coordinate with the IFLA/PAC Regional Centres, ICA, and UNESCO.

Other Cooperative Projects

Three recent cooperative efforts are worth noting here: the European Confederation of Conservator-Restorers' Organizations (ECCO), the Getty Conservation Institute/St. Petersburg project, and the Association for the Conservation of the Cultural Patrimony of the Americas (APOYO).

ECCO brings together representatives of conservation organizations in the EC, though it plans to liaise with conservation organizations throughout Europe and other parts of the world. Several working groups have been established, including one on education (*Abbey Newsletter* 15.7 [Nov. 1991]: 105).

The Getty Conservation Institute (GCI), in consultation with the Library of Congress, is establishing a Conservation Center in St. Petersburg with the Russian Academy of Sciences Library and the Russian National Library. The Center, still in the planning stages, will include a training component, and possibly exchange programs (Discussions with Ann Russell and others, Fall 1993).

The Association for the Conservation of the Cultural Patrimony of the Americas recently co-sponsored a seminar with the Getty Conservation Institute, the Library of Congress, and the Conservation Analytical Laboratory of the Smithsonian Institution. Entitled "Preventive Conservation in Latin America," the seminar was held in Washington, D.C. in August 1993. One of the core themes that ran through the meetings was the need for training in both practical and philosophical issues. Participants felt that training is needed at the professional and technical levels. Although APOYO may initially seek the support for training from international organizations, the long-term goal is to have a network of skilled individuals in each country who can then train others--a goal which we have already seen articulated by UNESCO for its own training efforts (Raphael, "Preventive Conservation," 67).

The 1990s may prove to be the decade of cooperative programs. The groundwork for international training has been laid by IFLA, UNESCO, GCI (see the GCI, *Training Program Activities, 1985-1991*), ICA, and more recently by the Commission on Preservation and Access. With the development of new initiatives by ECCO, APOYO, and GCI, and with the possibility of government support for cultural exchange programs through the EC and possibly NAFTA, the next few years could be productive for the dissemination of preservation education.

Individual Programs

". . . [E]ach country should have an agreed focal point for coordinating awareness campaigns, education and training" for preservation and conservation, concluded Alexander Wilson in his 1988 report, *Library Policy for Preservation and Conservation in the European Community* (60). While such a recommendation may seem logical, in practice such centralization may not always be possible. For example, as we saw in chapter 2, the preservation movement in the U. S. is decentralized yet still effective. And the United States is not alone in its decentralization; conservation and preservation efforts in countries such as Italy take place not only in libraries and archives, but in conservation centers such as the Istituto Centrale per la Patología del Libro (questionnaire from Maria Lilli di Franco, 2/2/93). A more realistic goal may be for individual programs in one country to coordinate some activities with one another.

An excellent description of a number of programs, both centralized and decentralized, can be found in *Education and Training for Preservation and Conservation,* the collected papers of the International Seminar on "The Teaching of Preservation Management for Librarians, Archivists, and Information Scientists" (edited by Josephine Riss Fang and Ann Russell) which was held in Vienna April 11-13, 1986, immediately following the "Preservation of Library Materials" conference held at the National Library of Austria, April 7-10, 1986. The presentations contained descriptions of library school programs in the Philippines and Nigeria, as well as teaching programs in national libraries. Rather than replicate what was presented there, I will discuss some general approaches.

There are several venues for teaching conservation and preservation (Table A). In some countries (e.g. Denmark and Germany) there are schools of conservation which are completely distinct from library schools (questionnaire from Hans Pedersen, 11/12/92). In other countries (e.g. Ghana and Sierra Leone) hands-on skills are taught in library schools (Questionnaire from S.K. Agyei, 11/17/92 and interview with Gladys Jusu-Sheriff, 8/20/93). Such training is vital in the education of librarians who need to undertake hands-on work. In England, there seems to be a consensus that scientific and technical training do not belong in library schools where the emphasis is on management (Interview with John Feather, 8/3/92). In the United States, the University of Texas offers programs in both conservation and preservation administration.

Some countries offer conservation and preservation training through programs of continuing education. In Hungary, as in many countries, there is no full-time training program for book and/or paper conservators. Some courses are offered at the Academy of Fine Arts, and since 1981 the National Library has offered joint evening courses in conservation with a specialized school of fine and applied arts. The training is conducted by both the school and the library. The hands-on component of the courses is given in the conservation workshops of the National Library. The courses last from two to two-and-a-half years depending on the backgrounds of the students (Kastaly, "Preservation and Conservation," 30).

In Greece, one can study conservation at the Department of Archaeological and Fine Arts Conservation of the Technological Educational Institute's School of Graphic and Art Studies. Students can specialize in books and paper. For preservation, librarians must turn to continuing education offerings because Greek library schools do not include preservation courses in their curricula. Continuing education seminars on the preservation of library and archival materials are offered by public and municipal libraries. The seminars vary from ten hours to four months (Skepastianu, "Preservation and Conservation," 8).

For the most part, there is more activity in national libraries than in library schools, though several library school programs have recently added preservation components including the University of New South Wales and the University of Toronto (interviews with Paul Wilson, 12/15/92, and Karen Turko, 12/9/93).

Regional centers, another venue for workshops and internships, are uncommon outside of the United States. If the GCI/St. Petersburg center is successful, it might stimulate to establishment of other centers. The St. Petersburg program, however, is distinct from U.S. centers in that it will serve only one city. In the U.S. centers usually serve a wider geographical area, and some centers will provide services anywhere in the country. There is a consortium of U.S. regional centers called the Association of Regional Conservation Centers (ARCC). The executive directors of the centers meet several times a year to work on cooperative projects. Recently, ARCC was awarded a challenge grant from the Mellon Foundation to establish a cooperative endowment. It is clear that the broad geographical areas that will be helped by this association was one of its appealing features for the granting agency. Cooperation which helps a widely distributed constituency is more likely to be funded than a single conservation or preservation project localized in one institution.

The panoply of approaches presented here demonstrates the ingenuity of educators in responding to local limitations and to various opportunities. For example, in countries that do not have conservation programs, library schools may be the logical place to teach hands-on skills. Or in places where library schools do not cover preservation or conservation, training programs might be provided by libraries. Once the need for education has been recognized, librarians and archivists have found a variety of ways to provide it. Through international cooperation, local programs can be enhanced. Individuals can do internships in other countries, or learn more about current practices through workshops.

This chapter has examined a number of educational initiatives. In closing, I would like to differentiate between three terms which are often used interchangeably, *training*, *education*, and *continuing education*, which are overlapping yet distinct concepts. *Training* usually implies the learning of specific or specialized skills, often in a workshop setting; for example, disaster recovery, care of photographic prints, book repairs, or monitoring the library environment.

Education is a more comprehensive term which refers not only to acquiring skills, but also to obtaining knowledge through experience, creativity, analysis, and the exchange of ideas. Education is life-long while training takes place over a finite period of time. *Continuing education* can take place at any stage of one's career. It may consist of refresher courses, or may lead to certificates of advanced study. Library schools, libraries, and professional associations offer continuing education programs.

Training workshops and courses are the most common form of educational opportunity offered by organizations such as IFLA. This is because short courses are relatively easy to set up, and there will always be a demand for them. However, training does not go too far; once people have acquired basic skills there is still much more to learn. Training courses cannot educate a student—because of their brevity—as thoroughly as a comprehensive program can.

Librarians and archivists have tended to focus on solving immediate problems such as what to do with brittle books. Such an approach is necessary, but it must not overshadow an equally important need: to prepare members of our profession to undertake the research they need to solve their problems. The kind of learning environment that makes research possible is the university, with is vast resources.

On an international level we must plan not only programs of training but more programs of research. We must find increasingly effective ways to disseminate the results of our work and to share our ideas. With the electronic and satellite technologies I described in chapter 7, it is already possible for universities and other institutions to link up with one another. Ideally, professionals around the world will be able not only to acquire whatever skills or knowledge they need, from basic workshops to graduate degrees, but also to work collaboratively on research as well. The problems that preservation and conservation aim to solve are ubiquitous and global. The solutions, then, must be equally universal. If politicians look to cooperation between nations to solve political problems, those in the library world must have a similar international approach. Cooperation will speed us all on our preservation mission.

4. The Preservation of Nonbook Formats: Implications for Education

As information is stored increasingly in electronic formats, as the very concept of the form and substance of the book is changing, it is time to re-examine the principles of preservation under which many of us, throughout the world, were trained and under which we are still guided in our decision making and in our teaching. These principles need to be compared to recent technological advances in the formation and storing of texts so that points of convergence or divergence can be evaluated. Only then can we hold fast to the old principles or develop new ones.

One can argue that preservation dates back to the origin of written records. In ancient times preservation consisted primarily of protecting items from all kinds of human and natural enemies by placing them in protective containers. Once libraries were established, the three broad areas of librarianship were acquisitions, the organization of texts (for access), and guardianship, which implies preservation of the collection. (The circulation of library materials is a relatively recent development in library history.) Yet although preservation has always been one of the primary aspects of librarianship, it has only become a recognized specialty within the library profession in recent times, as I discussed in chapter 1. In other words, storage, safekeeping, and repair of library materials have always been integral parts of librarianship but these activities were not formally designated as *preservation* until about a hundred years ago.

As the preservation of library materials became a specialization within librarianship, certain principles evolved which grew out of the guardianship mandate of librarianship, the discipline of bibliography, and the art conservation field. The guardianship aspect of librarianship is the assumption that, generally speaking, once research libraries acquire books, they are kept permanently. The second assumption is that the books will be stored in buildings that are structurally sound and secure; these buildings are usually owned, rented, or leased by the library or the institution to which the library belongs. Therefore the books are "owned" by the library. This is an important assumption to keep in mind, for in today's electronic environment, the ownership of texts by libraries can no longer be assumed or expected.

Regardless of how one defines bibliography, the study of it goes back centuries. For the purpose of this discussion, it is adequate simply to state that the value of particular books has been recognized for a long time. These books have been valued for such attributes as their artifactual, historical, or associational significance. There is a long tradition of appreciating books as artifacts where the underlying assumption is that *each* book requires special care and handling.

The influence of art conservation has been prevalent in the bibliographical approach to book conservation. It also lies in the artifactual one-by-one approach to treating items, and in the principle that, whenever possible, conservation treatments should be reversible.[1] This influence can be seen in the book conservation program which was developed at Columbia University; but the artifactual approach is also taught at other places such as the Istituto Centrale per la Patologia del Libro in Rome, and the Konservatorskolen at the Royal Danish Academy of Fine Arts in Copenhagen, to give just three examples.

From the artifactual approach the following broad conservation and preservation principles have evolved:

- When materials are treated, the treatments should, when possible, be reversible.[2]
- Whenever possible or appropriate, the originals should be preserved. Only materials that are untreatable should be reformatted.
- Library materials should be preserved for as long as possible.

These principles have come increasingly into conflict with the enormity of the library preservation problem: many millions of deteriorating books. (If the Greek myths were being written today, Sisyphus and Tantalus would be joined by Papirothus—the mean librarian who is eternally punished by acquiring ever more transient forms of the book.) The sheer size of the problem, as well as the high cost, has led us away from the artifactual approach towards such measures as mass deacidification and reformatting. These approaches have meant that more *texts* could be preserved. However, the effects of deacidification are not necessarily reversible, and in the case of reformatting programs, some institutions discard the books once they have been reformatted. So two of the three principles have already diminished in importance. The third is open to interpretation: should the objects be preserved for as long as possible, or should we preserve only the texts?

---

[1] The principles of longevity and reversibility are part of the *Code of Ethics and Standards of Practice* which deal specifically with conservation treatment issues. Originally drafted in 1963 when The American Institute for Conservation of Historic & Artistic Works was the International Institute for Conservation of Historic & Artistic Works--American Group, the Code has been revised several times (see the *AIC Directory* for more information). The Code is currently under revision again. AIC principles have influenced both conservators and preservation administrators.

[2] Actually, many conservators have argued that no treatment is truly reversible. So reversibility has come to mean that inasmuch as possible conservators will use the least intrusive treatments available. For example, thirty years ago lamination was a common method of strengthening documents. Today conservators are more likely to encapsulate an item.

The Preservation Problem

The use of mass deacidification and reformatting *assumes* that the items to be treated are paper-based to begin with. The environment in which we now find ourselves is replete with new media such as audio and video tapes, or computer and optical disks, all of which are constantly changing like Proteus. In some instances, for example with e-mail, the electronic format is the first and only format unless we print out the information. We are shifting from information in relatively permanent formats to information conveyed in formats so transitory that it can disappear at the stroke of a command key. Kurzweil (all cited articles) presents a world in which the "book" is a PC, telephone, television, and cybernetic research assistant all in one. Though he says that the electronic book ". . . falls short in some of the characteristics of paper and ink in areas of flicker, contrast, resolution, and color . . ., computer technology is anything but static, and already some of these limitations are being overcome" (Kurzweil, "The Future, . . . Part 2," p. 141).

More immediate than the Kurzweil "powerbooks" are the electronic formats already available in our libraries, for example, digital media such as CD-ROMs. These media have become an integral part of our library collections and yet they are deteriorating at a rate much quicker than originally thought (DeWhitt, "Long-Term Preservation, Part I," p. 7; Stielow, "Biting the WORM," p. 10). However, Lesk reminds us that perhaps of more import than deterioration is the fact that from now on data will have to be frequently "refreshed" (reformatted) because of technological obsolescence, e.g. the equipment used to convey information will be obsolete or cease to be manufactured as vendors go bankrupt or, themselves move on to more sophisticated storage media. "On the good side, the intervention of machinery between the actual object and the reader means that the users are unlikely to become emotionally attached to particular physical media, and thus reformatting of advanced technology should not produce the objections that accompany reformatting of books" (Lesk, p. 3).

In an ideal world where time, manpower, and money exist in equal shares, such regular reformatting could be expected. In the meantime, a lot of valuable information is disappearing, particularly in government archives. Sniffen has described information such as American census data, which has been lost because it is stored only on old computer tape from discarded systems (Sniffen, "Lost in Tapes," p. 46). Anderson describes administrative records from the 1980s "created in machine-readable form and . . . stored on media which at best had only a few years of reliable life and at worst were subject to regular overwritings in the interests of economy of data storage" (Anderson, "The Preservation," p. 79).

How do our principles hold up to these situations?

We can evaluate the principles in the context of the life cycle of information which consists of three stages: creation, life (or use), and disposal (reformatting, replacement, or disposal with no form of replacement). Preservation administrators are concerned with all of these stages.

The Life Cycle of Information

The deterioration of an item begins during creation. For books, deterioration is caused by many things, among which are poor methods of manufacture such as adding alum-rosin sizing to paper pulp, the use of sulfuric acids to accelerate the leather tanning process, and so on. In recent years the preservation community worldwide has lobbied paper manufacturers to produce permanent/durable papers, and the publishing industry to use such papers and to designate that use with an infinity sign on the verso of title pages. Nevertheless, even though some manufacturers can guarantee 250 years of life for their papers, all organic materials will disintegrate eventually, so there is ultimately a limit to what we can do.

The useful life of library materials can be extended not only through proper methods of manufacture, but by improving conditions of storage and use. Controlling the environments of buildings, proper shelving, and careful handling of materials will make them last longer. Preservation administrators have made great strides in extending the use of library materials, and in educating manufacturers, librarians, and users.

Finally, disposal may take place when individual items deteriorate beyond the possibility or practicality of repair. Replacement with a like item (assuming one exists), with reprints, or by reformatting are all solutions. (This stage usually requires collaborative decision-making with other librarians as well as with the vendors who can provide the necessary services.)

How does the life cycle differ for new media?
Creation: At this point, the preservation community has less knowledge and expertise about the development and manufacture of new formats than it does about more familiar formats such as paper. Also, physical durability of new media is not the ultimate problem, but rather *obsolescence*. Therefore, preservation administrators will have to plan for an ongoing process of media conversion, beginning at the point of acquisition.
Life: Storage conditions can be controlled for some new media *but not all electronic information is replicable*, and therefore it is not in a physical form which can be stored or saved. Librarians will need to decide *what* will be stored, *how* and *when* it will be stored, and by *whom*--the library, the creator, the end-user, or the publisher (the issue of how information could be stored and transmitted is examined by Fiddes and Winterbottom).

Reformatting will also be an integral part of this stage. Four areas of concern in media conversion are: 1) fragility (the inherent strength or inherent weakness of each medium), 2) rapidity of obsolescence of the operating apparatus of each medium, 3) the ease of altering documents (the ability to manipulate, change, or reformat data easily), and 4) proprietary rights and preservation (who owns the information, and who will take responsibility for its preservation--an area potentially more complex than copyright issues).

Disposal: Content or format--which will we preserve? To a certain extent these decisions will be market-driven. No matter how much people may resist initially, they will eventually give up their LP collections in favor of CDs which they will then only collect until the next technology comes along. We only have so much control over formats and will have to focus on content. Yet we must also realize that in changing formats something of the original is lost. The CD version of the Beethoven piano sonatas performed by Artur Schnabel may sound cleaner and crisper than the original LPs, but they also sound more sterile--some of the original atmosphere is gone. Gone too is an element in the evolution of the history of recorded sound.

Given these new scenarios, let us look at the principles of longevity and the importance of the artifact. There is no doubt, given the current technological environment of the late twentieth century, that the notion of both are changing radically. New technologies last a shorter time than do the older ones: papyrus, paper, vellum, vinyl records, etc. So much for the artifact; under these circumstances preservation administrators will have to be more concerned with the longevity of the information.

However, even as some new materials are being created only in electronic formats, what about the hundreds of millions of books currently housed in our libraries? And what of all the new materials which are still being published in the paper-book form? Most of these books will not disappear in our lifetimes. Preservation managers will need to continue to use established methods for the maintenance of these materials.

Yet the emergence of electronic information will result in a fundamentally different way of approaching our field which has been object-based (books, broadsides, maps, etc.) and time-oriented (e.g., permanent/durable paper should last at least 250 years). Thus the notion of saving object X for Y years may become obsolete. We will need to secure the longevity of information so that the information itself does not disappear. And it must be done in concert with librarians, publishers, manufacturers, and anyone else involved in the handling of the information. Malinconico makes an articulate plea for library educators to teach students how to cooperate with the whole community of individuals who are involved with the dissemination of information: computer and telecommunications specialists, vendors, community service agencies, and educational organizations, so that there is an understanding of the problems from all perspectives (Malinconico, "What Librarians Need," pp. 233-34).

Lesk (p. 16) also calls for cooperation but cites as his reason the technical aspects of the digital world. But such cooperation is already an integral part of the preservation field: deacidification, standards for microfilming, and other developments required collaboration among preservation managers, conservators, scientists, and corporations. The only difference in the digital world is that we may need to look more towards industry in our collaborative efforts.

There are a number of interesting initiatives currently under way that suggest more than one alternative. Some projects are sponsored by the Commission on Preservation and Access and the British Library. A description of these will give the reader some idea of the directions in which librarians, researchers, and corporations are headed.

The Commission on Preservation and access, since its formation in 1986, has been charged with creating a structure to set the conditions for a national preservation program. Since then it has sponsored research, organized task forces and symposia, and published numerous technical reports. And as I discussed in Chapters 2 and 3, international programs have become more central to its mission.

It has succeeded in accomplishing so much because it is an independent organization funded by universities, foundations, and granting organizations. It is an example of a network, a way of organizing activities that according to Naisbitt (*Megatrends,* pp. 192-94) is largely replacing the old hierarchies. In the case of preservation, it has emerged as an alternative to the more hierarchical programs found in national libraries. Without the burden of a large institutional hierarchy, the Commission has had the freedom to pursue a number of initiatives. The Commission's method of organizing a variety of activities through networks may well turn out to be the model that will be followed for some time to come.

Perhaps the most striking example of the Commission's networking has been through the work of Hans Rütimann who is International Project Consultant to the Commission. Through Rütimann's extensive travels he has reported on a variety of preservation initiatives (see bibliography).

The Technology Assessment Advisory Committee of the Commission has conducted and authored several pieces of research (e.g. Waters & Weaver). One of the members of the Committee, M. Stuart Lynn, Vice President of Information Technologies at Cornell University, is also involved in a collaborative effort between Cornell and Xerox (with some support from the Commission) to test a prototype system for recording the text of deteriorating books as digital images. High-quality and archivally sound paper facsimiles can be produced on demand from the digital images. The project is evaluated by Kenney and Personius. More recently Cornell has also experimented with digital-to-microfilm conversion; this research has been described by Kenney.

The British Library Research and Development Department sponsors its own research into electronic storage and transmission of texts.[3] One of these projects examined the feasibility of acquiring data for storage in an electronic archive directly from the printer after it was typeset into electronic form. The text could be acquired in ASCII code, which is compact. This way, the British Library could maintain an accessible record of the intellectual content of published works. The user would have access to the information online. In order to determine the feasibility of such a plan, two researchers undertook a survey of printers to ascertain current technology and practices in Britain. The study concluded that it should be possible to convert much of the text held in electronic form (Fiddes and Winterbottom, "The Feasibility," pp. 1-2).

The purpose of all the projects described here is to capture the information, store it centrally, and then make it available to users on demand. The emphasis is on the information itself rather than on the artifact.

There is still another approach to the preservation of nonbook formats, one in which we treat the new formats as objects, much as we have treated books, archives, maps, and so on. Some of the preservation literature describes storage, handling, and use of various formats; this literature is becoming more voluminous every day. To cite just two recent examples, St-Laurent has written *The Care and Handling of Recorded Sound Materials* which discusses the physical characteristics of these formats, how they deteriorate, and how best to minimize their deterioration. The Image Permanence Institute has published *Storage Guide for Acetate Film* which not only provides information about optimum storage conditions, but helps the reader predict the effects of actual film storage on the life expectancy of film collections. As libraries acquire more formats they will depend increasingly on such literature.

After spending considerable time in this complex information environment, where will we find ourselves? And which principles will be practiced? Will books be treated as museum objects are today, as rare items because in the future so few will be manufactured? Will reversibility become a dead issue because we will no longer expect our information objects to last hundreds of years? Will our very concept of permanence change in the next generation as consumer goods become disposable at an even faster rate than today's average paperback book? The answer to most of these questions is likely to be "yes." Our concepts will change as the places in which we work change. But our commitment to preserving information for future generations will certainly remain. And it is that philosophical commitment which we as library school educators must communicate to our students.

---

[3] My knowledge of these projects is based in part on my discussion of them with Terry Cannon held at the Research and Development Department of the British Library on 7/29/92.

The Law of the Situation

Naisbitt (pp. 85-86) and Kurzweil ("The Future. . ., Part 3," p. 63) refer to the Law of the Situation which asks "what business are you really in?" The Law was formulated in 1904 by Mary Parker Follet, the first management consultant in the U. S. (Follet, *The Giving of Orders*, pp. 58-59). The question is usually asked when the business environment changes and a company or industry must reconceptualize its mission, though Follett saw it as applicable to all organizations. Naisbitt uses the railroads as an example of an industry that did not understand the Law of the Situation. Instead of seeing themselves in the transportation business they saw themselves only as railroads and almost became obsolete.

Kurzweil uses the blacksmith at the turn of the century as a metaphor for the position that libraries and other public institutions are in today. The blacksmith who saw himself as a facilitator of transportation traded in his forge for a gas pump. Kurzweil contends that if libraries see their mission broadly as gathering information and making it universally available (not confined by library buildings or adversely influenced by current perceptions of librarianship), then they will become even more important in time (Kurzweil, "The Future . . ., Part 3," p. 63).

Applying the Law of the Situation to the field of preservation, we must consider the primary underpinnings of what we do. Are we ultimately concerned with the preservation of individual items, or of the preservation of knowledge? If the former, then our field will merely respond to changes brought about by each new technology. If the latter, then we must help to shape the sources that will create and distribute information. It must be both: we must continue to save as much information as possible regardless of the format it is in or the means by which it is stored and disseminated.

5. Resources for Preservation Education

> **resource 1.** something that can be used for support or help: *the local library is a valuable resource.* **2.** Often **resources.** An available supply that can be drawn on when needed. **3.** The ability to deal with a difficult or troublesome situation effectively; initiative: *a person of resource.* **4.** Often **resources.** Means that can be used to cope with a difficult situation: *needed all my intellectual resources for the exam.* **5. a. resources.** The total means available for economic and political development, such as mineral wealth, labor force, and armaments. (*The American Heritage Dictionary of the English Language.* 3rd ed. Boston: Houghton Mifflin, 1992, p. 1536.)

The field of preservation depends on a variety of resources. Although the word *resources* is often associated with financial support, it has multiple denotations and connotations, as the above definitions illustrate. This brief chapter will consider three types of resources: monetary, individual, and material, all of which overlap. These three constitute the range of possibilities available for the development of new and the continuation of existing preservation education programs.

Monetary Resources

It is natural to equate resources with money; after all, without money how can a program of any kind be sustained? A program requires staff, space, equipment, books, and supplies. Money is necessary for all of these, yet it will take a program only so far. Without the commitment to an ongoing educational program, books will languish on the shelves, and classrooms will remain empty. Money is but one link in the preservation education chain.

Some library directors and deans have become interested in preservation only because grant money has been available in recent years. If the institution's administrators perceive that they must commit short- or long-term funds to preservation, they may be disinclined to do so unless the preservation specialists are successful advocates for the place of preservation programs in that institution. Also, a program based entirely on external funding will probably disappear as soon as the money does. Therefore it is important to build a program through a variety of resources, with some level of permanent support from the institution's operating budget.

If the commitment to preservation is strong, but the monetary resources weak, a library director or dean must evaluate both the available and the needed resources. In a library school setting, for example, staff resources might already exist in the faculty. Fundraising efforts might focus on scholarships, books and other teaching materials. Or, if no one on the faculty can teach preservation, the library school might line up an adjunct professor from the library in the same university, or someone nearby whose presence will not cost the university travel or per diem expenses. If the adjunct faculty member is employed by a corporation, the employer might grant her release time for teaching. At some universities employees cannot be paid more than 100% time. So to teach a course in one's own institution may not be financially rewarding for an adjunct. Other incentives—perhaps altruistic—might attract a potential adjunct. Or, the library school may pay back the adjunct faculty member with a graduate student assistant, or other benefit. Deans and directors may work together to create any number of paybacks. These arrangements take advantage of individual (human) resources. Since many granting agencies require cost sharing on the part of the recipient institution, staff time may be a significant program component.

Over the past fifteen years, funding for preservation has come from a number of sources: international bodies (e.g. UNESCO); government agencies; universities; national libraries; private foundations (e.g. Getty, Mellon, Rockefeller, Volkswagen); corporations (e.g. publishing houses, commercial binderies, suppliers such as La Reliure Administrative, and companies specializing in the reproduction of texts such as Xerox); professional associations (e.g. IFLA and the International Council on Archives, ICA); and, cooperative and collaborative initiatives (e.g. a national library with a university; a corporation with a university or universities; The Commission on Preservation and Access with IFLA's Preservation and Conservation Regional Centres); and, individuals (e.g. Barbara Goldsmith, Trustee, New York Public Library).

In Germany, funding for education and culture takes place mostly at the state and local levels. The federal government tends to be interested only in far-reaching cultural programs such as the Goethe Institute. Some states generate cultural funds from lotteries, soccer pools, and gambling casinos (Dornberg, "Germany: Pride and Patronage," 100). Unfortunately, there are no statistics on how much of these monies goes to preservation and conservation.

For less developed countries, organizations such as UNESCO have provided assistance through fellowships, publications, and the establishment of library schools. In 1990, the Judy Segal Trust was established in memory of the senior paper conservator at the Bodleian Library in Oxford who died in 1989. The trust awards grants in two areas which were of particular interest to her: the training of conservators, and the conservation needs of libraries and archives in less developed countries (*Abbey Newsletter*, 16.4 [August 1992]: 64).

Although individuals have not yet become major contributors to preservation programs, gifts from individuals (including bequests) account for 90% of all charitable giving in the United States (figure quoted in Steele and Elder, 29). As foundation and governmental funding for preservation levels off, individual giving will become a more important source for preservation programs.

But generating such gifts requires considerable work; it is not as straightforward as applying for a grant. It may take years to develop a relationship with a potential donor. Some libraries and library schools have development officers with whom the preservation educator will work closely. Together the preservation and development specialists can develop an effective fundraising strategy. In some cases the preservation specialist may even need to identify donors with a particular interest in preservation so as not to compete with other programs for some of the same donors.

The need for preservation and conservation has become more familiar to people worldwide in recent years, often because of wars, natural disasters brought about by floods, earthquakes, hurricanes, and tornadoes, vandalism of various kinds, or environmental hazards such as global warming. The media often catch the destruction of museums and libraries on camera or in still photography which is then relayed around the world. This makes people aware that our cultural heritage is vulnerable. The sight of damaged books or works of art sets off an emotional response and individuals often send monetary contributions to libraries and museums immediately after a disaster. In the United States, the Division of Preservation and Access of the National Endowment for the Humanities makes emergency funds available to institutional collections which have suffered damage as a result of a disaster. Federal emergency funds are also available in many countries; in the United States the Federal Emergency Management Agency (FEMA) is such an organization. FEMA also offers an educational service via the satellite Emergency Educational Network (Roberts, "Establishing a Disaster Prevention/Response Plan," 17.)

On the international level, we are in the third year of the United Nations International Decade for Natural Disaster Reduction (IDNDR). Four of the five goals of the IDNDR exemplify the types of resource sharing delineated above. Briefly, these four are: "2) to devise appropriate guidelines and strategies for applying existing knowledge, taking into account the cultural and economic diversity among nations; 3) to foster scientific and engineering endeavors aimed at closing critical gaps in knowledge in order to reduce loss of life and property; 4) to disseminate existing and new information related to measures for assessment, prediction, prevention, and mitigation of natural disasters; and 5) to develop measures for the assessment, prediction, prevention, and mitigation of natural disasters through programs of technical assistance and technology transfer, demonstration projects, and education and training, tailored to specific hazards and locations, and to evaluate the effectiveness of those programs" (Roberts, 15). These efforts will require not only monetary, but individual, and material resources as well. It is envisioned that each country will undertake its own National Decade for Natural Disaster Reduction while cooperating with other countries. Over the course of the decade, publications will be issued which will include information about existing disaster mitigation strategies, a roster of disaster mitigation experts, training modules, and programs.

One of the results of the 1986 Los Angeles, California Public Library fire was the formation of the Los Angeles Preservation Network (LAPNet). LAPNet—which is organized by a steering committee and has a mailing list of some 500 librarians, archivists, and curators—maintains a list of disaster-related services and suppliers. It also puts on several workshops and programs per year on topics such as book repairs, salvage techniques, reformatting, and so on. LAPNet mainly serves the greater Los Angeles county area; following LAPNet's lead, librarians in Orange, Riverside, and other southern California counties have organized their own networks.

The LAPNet meetings and plans have yielded a large cadre of trained volunteers. The training opportunities that have emerged from LAPNet's efforts can serve as a model in other regions of the world. The key here is that fundraising for *education* may be linked with fundraising for the actual conservation work that needs to be undertaken after a disaster. Those who are raising funds for preservation education should be alert to this possibility.

In the absence of disasters, fundraisers need to develop strategies in order to attract individual donors to preservation. In *Becoming a Fundraiser*, Steele and Elder suggest that "donors give to satisfy their needs rather than the library's needs, and donors' needs usually involve projects that will 'make a difference' rather than projects designed to maintain already established resources. . ." (31). For preservation education, potential fundraising efforts might focus on a scholarship fund, an endowed professorial chair, or a lecture series. Any of these could be named funds. Naming a scholarship fund or a lecture series may encourage continued support from a particular individual or attract others who might also like to see their names associated with preservation.

Whatever the source of the funding, successful preservation programs will continue to draw on every available resource, monetary and otherwise.

Individual Resources

At a fall 1993 preservation-related meeting in Los Angeles, talk inevitably turned to the recent fires which struck Malibu, Laguna, and other southern California communities. We were all amused to learn that each one of us had been prepared to help with salvage efforts if needed. And I do mean *prepared.* Several of us keep emergency kits in our offices containing flashlights, boots, plastic bags, tools, and old clothing. In 1986 hundreds of volunteers helped salvage damaged materials from the Los Angeles Public Library after an arson fire (in fact the Library reopened in the fire-damaged building only in October 1993). Between earthquakes and fires, the threat of disasters is always looming in southern California, and curators and librarians are well-prepared.

LAPNet is an example of an organization that is run entirely on a volunteer basis. There are no dues, and the minimal monetary support that it needs is provided by the institutions in which the steering committee members work. Additional funds have come from the sale of the disaster supplier list and the workshops that LAPNet runs. LAPNet's greatest resource is its membership who provide the labor, skills, and ideas which keep LAPNet an active and innovative organization.

Networking has long been a technique used in the United States to disseminate information and provide training, as I discussed in chapter 2. Through international organizations and electronic modes of communication networking will certainly continue to expand; this is discussed at length in chapter 7.

The fields of preservation and conservation have long had a core of individuals who have volunteered their time and energy. Such expertise was galvanized after the Florence, Italy, floods in 1966 when librarians and conservators from all over the world converged there to help with the salvage efforts. The results of the interaction between conservators and other volunteers resulted in new salvage and treatment techniques which have been amply chronicled in journals, dissertations, and books (e.g., Darling/Ogden and Peter Waters). The experience also led to the development of training programs at the Biblioteca Nazionale in Florence, the Library of Congress, and Trinity College, Dublin.

Preservation and conservation expertise exists worldwide; it could be put to use through faculty exchanges, an increase in the number of internship programs, network exchanges, and the development of distance learning programs developed specifically for preservation. (Distance learning programs have already been established by several library schools, but none of the programs yet offers a preservation specialization.)

Material Resources

Material resources include institutions; the people who work there; laboratories and classrooms; books, documents, and artifacts; tools and technologies. Material resources are built up over a long period of time. They can be replicated or modified from one institution to another. Material resources are the foundation for all programs. For example, a university has classrooms, laboratories, great collections of library materials, personnel who are teachers and researchers, publishing capabilities, and so on. Non-human resources may be available throughout a university campus and even outside the campus, such as an online library catalog, or electronic mail.

We use these resources in our daily work, but the resources may also be further reaching. A researcher in country A uses the online catalog from country D; someone in country M puts on a workshop using a government document (which may be freely copied since it is not copyrighted) published in country X. All of these resources can be used in the development of preservation education programs.

Over the past thirty years funding for preservation has experienced the same vicissitudes as funding for the arts and education: there was a boom in the 1960s and a recession in the seventies which was then followed by a smaller boom in the eighties which has led to further recessions in the nineties. Given the global nature of the economy, recessions are worldwide with but a few exceptions. Each slowdown has inspired us to take advantage of all of our non-monetary resources. For example, staff layoffs may lead to the absorption of duties by other employees. The term "downsizing" is used with increasing frequency in corporations, universities, museums, and libraries. But for activities as important and essential as preservation and conservation, downsizing should not occasion a cessation or diminution of the education or practice of these disciplines. Such a reduction would imperil the preservation efforts of the world's cultural memory. This is the message that conservators and preservation specialists must impart to their administrators. If the institution is simply so strapped that it must cease to fund these needs, it may still be able to support preservation efforts through release time for staff continuing education opportunities, or it may be able to coordinate preservation activities with other institutions.

Preservation education can rise to the occasion by continuing to take advantage of all the resources at its disposal. Additionally, new technologies for education will make the dissemination of information easier. But we must recognize that not everyone in the world has access to these technologies, and education will have to continue to be provided in a variety of ways.

The shortage of monetary resources is creating many new collaborative efforts. For example, The Commission on Preservation and Access in its 1992-93 *Annual Report* announced that it would be working more closely with IFLA on the collaborative programs of the Preservation and Conservation Regional Centres (10). This international collaboration may inspire others. Certainly the work of the European Community (EC) in the promotion of permanent paper, if successful, might be replicated through the North American Free Trade Agreement (NAFTA) and other multi-national economic pacts.

In the meantime, libraries, museums, historical centers, library schools, regional networks, and other organizations are working hard to maintain programs which were well funded in the 1980s. Darwinism may prevail in the survival of programs. Yet for every program which ultimately fails, others will be revitalized, spurred on by the creativity that often prevails in lean economic times.

The next several years may demonstrate that preservation education can thrive because of the multiplicity of its resources, especially in the presence of all kinds of disasters, natural, man-made, and economic.

6. Research and Development

Conservation and preservation are interdisciplinary fields. A conservator must have a background in science as well as in art history and studio art. Knowledge about some aspects of engineering is also useful in working with HVAC systems in libraries, archives, and museums. Conservation, like architecture, brings together the disciplines of the humanities and the sciences.

Preservation has generally been taught in schools of library and information science, and librarianship is itself interdisciplinary, drawing from the humanities, social sciences, and computer sciences. The preservation administrator must be well versed in the various aspects of librarianship because preservation programs impact all the basic functions of libraries: technical services, collection development, circulation, special collections, interlibrary loans, reference and bibliographic instruction, building maintenance, general administration, and, increasingly, automation. Preservation administrators must also understand conservation principles as they relate to physical treatment options and the design of environmental systems, since few libraries and archives have both preservation administrators and conservators on staff.

The distinction between conservation and preservation is fuzzy to the layperson, and for good reason: the field of preservation grew out of conservation (as I discussed in chapter 1). Many preservation administrators began their careers as conservators (the author included). And some preservation administrators have gone on to study bookbinding, and other techniques of physical treatment. Today most libraries have preservation administrators but not conservators--items needing physical treatment tend to be sent out to private conservators or companies specializing in conservation work. At the same time, some smaller institutions have opted to hire conservators rather than preservation administrators. For this reason the Columbia (now Texas) programs require that preservation and conservation students obtain the library degree as well as the additional certificates in their own fields.

Because of the confluence of preservation and conservation, there are overlapping research domains, for example, research on mass deacidification and paper strengthening, and procedures for disaster recovery. But each field has its own specific concerns. Preservation literature, found mostly---though not entirely--in library publications is concerned with management issues, such as specifications for preservation microfilming, working with library binders, general library policy issues, and so on. In the conservation literature one will be more likely to find articles relating to treatment, e.g. on the use of bleach or enzymes. Articles on treatment may be too detailed or technical for the interests of a preservation administrator whose more immediate concerns have to do with budgeting, statistics, and other details of managerial life. This is not to suggest that conservators do not have to deal with administrative issues; they too apply for grants, write disaster recovery plans, and so on. But treatment is the thrust of conservation, and management is at the center of preservation.

Sometimes, however, conservators and preservation administrators have different perspectives. To a preservation administrator the term *reformatting* refers to the process of transferring text from one medium to another, such as converting a book to microform or optical disk. To a conservator, reformatting means the *alteration* not *transfer* of a physical object. Encapsulating a document, or removing maps or plates from a book and placing the removed items into flat storage are both examples of reformatting (Fredericks, *JAIC*, 96-97). The book that is microfilmed may be saved or discarded, but both scenarios constitute reformatting in the eyes of preservation administrators. In conservation, the text of the item being reformatted still exists, albeit in an altered form.

So how do the functions of preservation administration and book conservation influence research? Is there a clearly identifiable research base that is common to both fields? Who sponsors such research and where is it carried out?

First, let us consider what constitutes research in conservation and preservation and where it is published. We will then establish a research taxonomy (or categories) for each field. Next we will examine where the research is carried out and by whom, and where the resources come from.

Conservation Research

The field of conservation is concerned with effective, safe, and reversible methods of physical treatment. Research is carried out by conservators, conservation scientists, and other scientists who develop conservation-related techniques and products. The literature is published in journals such as *Studies in Conservation* (International Institute for Conservation of Historic and Artistic Works), *Museum* (UNESCO), *Restaurator* (Denmark), *The Paper Conservator* (Institute of Paper Conservation), *Maltechnic Restauro* (International Association for Conservation of Books, Paper and Archival Materials), *The Alkaline Paper Advocate* (U.S.), and *Journal of the American Institute for Conservation* and the related AIC Book and Paper Group publications *BPG Annual*, *Paper Conservation Annual*, and *Book Conservation Catalog*, to name a few. Also the Getty Conservation Institute and some regional conservation centers which have publishing arms publish monographs and leaflets. Many newsletters summarize the research published in journals and monographs, for example *The Abbey Newsletter: Bookbinding and Conservation*.

Conservation research fits into roughly four categories: 1) scientific research, 2) treatment methods, 3) historical research, and, 4) ethics. The examples given below are meant to be illustrative not exhaustive.

1. Scientific research

There are many scientific research projects focusing on every area of conservation. The categories I list here are for research on paper conservation. Categories could also be enumerated for inks, bookbinding, leather, and other areas of conservation research.

composition or chemical properties (e.g. fibers & fillers) determined through microscopy

composition or physical properties determined through visual inspection and testing, e.g. Elmendorf tear test

deterioration caused by inherent vice or poor environmental conditions, determined through accelerated or natural aging, simulated micro-environments

development of methods to retard deterioration washing and/or deacidification, fumigation, freezing

2. Treatment methods

Rapid advances in technology and science in the last dozen or so years have produced a myriad of new treatment methods for conservation of all library materials. I list here only examples for books and paper.

invasive

rebinding or rebacking; paper splitting, lamination, leafcasting

non-invasive

phase-boxing and other protective enclosures

collections conservation

environmental controls

3. Historical research

This work is concerned with tracing treatments that have been used at different times, for example preservatives used in pastes in the eighteenth century. Such information can be gleaned from contemporary trade manuals and may be useful in developing a course of treatment. (Unfortunately such source material is scant and not always reliable.) Historical research may also examine the methods used to manufacture materials, such as paper and leather, again using contemporary sources. Historical research is also carried out on bookbinding structures. This research is an example of how such inquiries can be applied to modern conservation techniques.

4. Ethics

Articles written in this area usually consider ethical standards which apply to treatment methods. For example, whether treatments are truly reversible, or when treatments constitute restoration rather than conservation.
Ethics may also refer to the concern with issues relating to the treatment and exhibition of sacred objects (see Chapter 1 and also the Spring 1992 issue of the *Journal of the American Institute for Conservation*).

The very definition of and context for ethics have been discussed in the *AIC Newsletter* over the past two years because a committee has undertaken the laborious task of rewriting AIC's ethical standards.

Conservation research is sponsored by the private and public sectors. In many countries there are research laboratories in the national archives, libraries, and museums. Some prominent examples are labs in the British Library, the National Archives of Canada, the Library of Congress (not technically a "national library" but one supported by the federal government), the Smithsonian Institution, 2the National Library of Australia, the National Diet Library of Japan, the Bibliothèque Nationale, and Die Deutsche Bibliothek which supports the Zentrum für Bucher Haltung (known to English-speakers as the Center for Book Preservation and Conservation, CBPC). In Italy, L'Istituto Centrale per la Patología del Libro (ICPL) is an autonomous center that is not directly connected to a library, but its director reports to the central office for libraries and cultural institutions (Wilson, *Library Policy*, 87).

Privately funded conservation centers and institutes also carry out research; the Getty Conservation Institute with its interest in enhancing conservation practice throughout the world is a prominent example. Regional conservation centers (e.g. Pacific Regional Conservation Center, Honolulu, Conservation Center for Art and Historic Artifacts, Philadelphia) may also develop new conservation techniques and publish articles or distribute leaflets describing them.

There are also self-supporting research centers within schools. Two American examples are the Institute of Paper Science and Technology which is affiliated with the Georgia Institute of Technology--though it is separately incorporated and has its own graduate program--and the Image Permanence Institute at the Rochester Institute of Technology. Both of these institutes carry out research which is funded by grants from government or private foundations, or by professional associations. For example, the National Information Standards Organization (NISO) commissioned the Institute of Paper Science and Technology to conducts tests on coated and uncoated papers (*Permanence of Paper for Publications*, vii), and the Library of Congress commissioned the Institute to perform tests on mass deacidification methods (telephone conversation with Martha Hill, Librarian at the Institute, 11/2/93). Similarly, the Image Permanence Institute is undertaking a study, supported by the New York State Project for the Conservation and Preservation of Library Research Materials, to investigate optimum storage conditions for color photographs (electronic mail message received 10/21/93 on the *Conservation Distribution List*).

Granting agencies such as the Mellon and the Volkswagen Foundations have provided funding for international research at some of the above-named institutions; the Getty Conservation Institute has also funded research, as has the Commission on Preservation and Access.

International organizations which try to coordinate research activities also exist. One example is the International Round Table on Audio-Visual Records, located in St. Albans, United Kingdom. The Round Table works in different areas of image and sound archiving. Among its members are the International Council on Archives (ICA) and IFLA (Child, *Directory*, 6).

Private industry will undertake conservation-related research if it results in a marketable product. In the area of deacidification, the Lithium Corporation of America developed the Lithco MG-3 process, Texas Alkyls implemented the DEZ process which was developed at the Library of Congress, and, for a time, Union Carbide manufactured Wei T'o (Cloonan, "Mass Deacidification," 98-99). It is important to keep in mind, however, that corporations will put money into development only if they feel that it will pay off for them in the long run. Products developed by corporations are proprietary and may disappear if a company goes out of business. Therefore this arena for conservation research is only of limited usefulness in a discussion of research in the context of education.

Notably absent from the types of institutions supporting conservation research is the university.
As I noted above, the Image Permanence Institute and the Institute of Paper Science and Technology are affiliated with institutes of technology. One would also expect to find the university, with its vast physical and intellectual resources, to be pre-eminent in such research. Why is it not? Probably for three reasons: 1) research is usually undertaken in specific graduate programs, e.g. public health, medical schools, chemistry departments. Yet there is only a handful of graduate programs in conservation and they tend to be small. Small programs with limited facilities and few sources for outside funding simply cannot get the support that larger schools can. A medical school can draw on federal support, and, for specific areas—say, cancer research—private sources as well. Additionally, cancer, an area which concerns and interests millions, inspires people to put on fund raisers. Cancer research also receives a lot of press. The conservation of material culture simply does not have that caché or perceived importance. So the academic institutions which stand to benefit from conservation research simply cannot raise the corporate and public interest—and therefore the money—to carry out such research. 2) The library would be a logical

venue for research on mass deacidification but university libraries do not have the facilities or funding for large-scale research—in fact they never have had. 3) University politics do not favor small research programs. Increasingly, at least in the United States and the United Kingdom, senior university administrators are beginning to view departments and schools as "cost centers." If individual units on campus have the opportunity to receive research grants, then those units are expected to be largely self-supporting.

There are notable exceptions to the bleak scenario which I have painted. Research for the British Library graft polymerization process to strengthen paper has been conducted at the University of Surrey. And research into new formats (discussed below under Preservation Research) is taking place at Cambridge University (Interview with Terry Cannon, July 29, 1992), and Cornell and Yale Universities. But generally, the economic climate for the 1990s does not seem to favor conservation research in universities. Preservation research, as we shall see below, will probably fare somewhat better.

Preservation Research

Preservation research is potentially diffuse; theoretically it could include all conservation research since preservation administrators may supervise conservation units. Confluences are particularly apparent in the areas of environmental controls and disaster recovery. Conservation literature tends to focus on techniques, e.g., the effects of the fumigant ethylene oxide or the use of freezing in insect control, while preservation literature focuses more on preventive or management issues: keeping food and drink out of the library. The research is undertaken by librarians, conservators with preservation responsibilities, and library school faculty.

Preservation research tends to be published in the library literature. In the United States these periodicals include *College & Research Libraries*, *Library Resources & Technical Services, Library Trends, Wilson Library Bulletin* (which recently inaugurated a preservation column), the *American Archivist*, *The New Library Scene,* and numerous other library journals which occasionally run preservation articles. There are also two publications devoted almost entirely to preservation: the *Abbey Newsletter* (which also includes conservation literature) and *Conservation Administration News*. In Europe some of the notable journals which run preservation articles are: the *Aslib* (Association for Information Management) *Proceedings*, *Libri*, *IFLA Journal*, *Journal of Librarianship*, and *Library Association Record*, *Restaurator*, though mostly concerned with conservation issues, also publishes articles of interest to preservation administrators.

In addition to the periodical literature, preservation publications emanate from international organizations and professional associations. UNESCO publishes the *Records and Archives Management Program (RAMP) Studies* as well as occasional monographs. These cover such topics as caring for collections in the tropics, disaster recovery procedures, and education for conservation and preservation. In the United

States, the Association of Research Libraries and the Commission on Preservation and Access publish reports, guides, and manuals. The Commission is making some of its publications available in Spanish for worldwide dissemination (Interview with Pat Battin, 11/16/92).

Preservation research can be divided into the following five broad areas: 1) the management of programs, 2) reformatting or transfer technologies, 3) the library environment and disaster recovery and prevention, 4) historical and bibliographical studies, and 5) general policy issues.

1. The Management of Programs

This research, often practical in nature, focuses on:

the functions of a preservation program (e.g. collection management, collection maintenance, circulation policies, library binding and repair, building maintenance)

designing user-education programs
planning models (such as self-studies, surveys, long-range planning)

funding (budgeting, cost models)

local, state-wide, national, and international programs

2. Reformatting or Transfer Technologies

This research focuses on feasibility, cost, implementation, cataloging, storage, and longevity issues relating to the transfer of library materials from one format to another. Examples include:

books to microform

digitization of books and microfilm the conversion of deteriorated books to digital images which can later be reconverted to permanent paper facsimiles on demand (Cornell/Xerox)

the transfer of sound recordings from one medium to another, e.g. records to compact disks

the transfer of moving images from one medium to another, e.g. film to videotape.

3. The Library Environment/Disaster Recovery and Prevention

This field overlaps with conservation research. The preservation literature, however, focuses more on such management issues as working with plant managers to insure optimal performance of HVAC systems, developing procedures for preventative maintenance through building inspections, integrated pest management, contracting with transportation companies and corporations with freezers for the shipping and storage of water-damaged materials, and so on.
In the area of disasters, the preservation literature focuses on developing recovery plans, training employees in recovery methods, or how individual libraries or archives recovered their materials after a disaster. One recent article even dealt with the kind of education that police, fireman, custodians, and administrators need *before* and *during* a disaster in order to teach others the best policies, record keeping, and handling techniques for treating damaged materials (Atkins and Belcher, "Coordinating a Bomb Blast Recovery").

4. Historical and Bibliographical Studies

Historical research examines the development of preservation programs (Higginbotham, *Our Past Preserved*) or influential individuals in the field (Crowe's dissertation on Verner Clapp). Bibliographical studies are centered on issues that relate to the artifact: how library materials are used by scholars or reformatting issues (Tanselle, "Reproductions and Scholarship"). Historical and bibliographical studies may focus on either conservation (treatment) or preservation (management) issues.

5. General Policy Issues

This literature covers everything from local library to national preservation policies. Some recent issues that have been addressed in the library literature include reformatting versus physical treatment of items; the pros and cons of mass deacidification; and, in the United States, the impact of shrinking acquisitions budgets and the concomitant rise in interlibrary loans on the physical condition of library materials.

Since so much of the preservation research is ultimately concerned with management issues, it is not expensive to undertake in the way that conservation research is, with its dependence on laboratories. Generally, libraries will underwrite the expenses that preservation administrators incur in carrying out their research such as computer time and the cost of statisticians. Similarly, library school faculty receive some university support. The notable exception, where research is expensive, is in the area of reformatting. Some of this research is being funded by the National Endowment for the Humanities (U.S.), the Mellon Foundation (U.S. and Europe), and the Commission on Preservation and Access (worldwide).

We have looked at the broad categories of conservation and preservation research, the types of organizations that have undertaken the research, and publications which have emanated from all of the above. Is there a clearly definable research base for both? What should the role of library schools be in supporting research in these areas?

Preservation and conservation have a common research goal: to develop the means for the preservation of the human record. The perspectives and foci brought to each discipline are different; preservation stresses management while conservation focuses on treatment. One depends on scientific research, the other on social science and humanistic research. But these differing means have the same end.

There is a clearly definable research base for both. Though these disciplines are themselves different, progress is made through the collaborative efforts of the preservation and conservation communities. For example, mass deacidification depends not only on the development of appropriate chemical treatments, but also on the selection of appropriate items for treatment and the ability of a preservation librarian to raise the funds for a deacidification program. Selection is based on physical criteria (will mass deacidification adversely affect plastic films? is the paper already too brittle?) and patterns of use (is this book a good candidate for microfilming?). Such determinations will come from a preservation administrator's research, in tandem with a conservator's advice and expertise. Therefore, the relationship between conservators, conservation scientists, and preservation administrators is symbiotic.

Should conservation and preservation research take place in library schools, libraries, and universities? Yes, though conservation and preservation research will continue to be carried out by government agencies and corporations too, much as medical research occurs in universities, government agencies, and drug companies. Universities cannot afford to fund all research, but they do have a responsibility to train students to carry it out. Universities also frame the research questions, and faculty play advisory roles to both the government and private sectors. Graduates may themselves work in a variety of settings. The university is at the core of the research nexus.

Conservation and preservation research will continue regardless of the ultimate fate of individual libraries or library schools. The continuation of research is more dependent on the survival of libraries and on the continuing recognition of the need to preserve artifacts and information than it is on the survival of any given school or academic program.

In preservation, practitioners have led educators, as I discussed in Chapter 2. It is now time for library school educators to lead practitioners--educators must be catalysts for change. This can be accomplished if library school educators foster doctoral-level education in both preservation and conservation and have an active role in already existing conservation and preservation research. Library schools should be producing imaginative researchers who can address the increasingly complex conservation and preservation problems that beset us.

7. The Dissemination of Information for Preservation Education

The many types of communication technologies in the world provide ample vehicles for the dissemination of information. We can teach with computer-based training courses, communicate with students via electronic mail, voice mail, or faxes, transmit our lectures throughout the world using satellite hook-ups, translate course materials using machine translation (MT), and almost instantly network with colleagues globally. This chapter will broadly assess these technologies and in so doing, address several questions. What are the components of preservation education? How is preservation information currently disseminated? Which components of preservation education lend themselves to new technologies? Who will benefit from new technological modes of communication? Who will be left out? Do new technologies enhance as well as increase educational opportunities?

In chapters 1 and 2, I described the evolution of conservation and preservation education. Today, educational opportunities are provided by library, polytechnic, and art schools, libraries, museums, historical societies, archives, and professional associations. The offerings include degree programs, individual courses, workshops, and internships. Most programs are based on in-person and hands-on approaches, though instructors may use slides, videotapes, or other audio-visual aids to augment their lectures and demonstrations.

However, the knowledge which is gained through these structured educational channels comprises but a small percentage of all the education which we as professionals receive throughout our careers. We spend significant amounts of time augmenting what we learned in school or in workshops. Most of the time, we obtain information (and ultimately, knowledge) through publications and informal sources such as the invisible college (see Table C). (By *invisible college* I mean the sharing of information among professionals through informal--usually oral--channels.) In "The Dissemination of Preservation Information," Merrily Smith describes the ways in which preservation professionals gather information. She points out that in some respects the informal communication channels such as conferences, telephone calls, e-mail, and gray literature (e.g. conference preprints, unpublished reports, other unpublished literature) have been more successful in disseminating information than journal and monograph publications. This has occurred for several reasons: subject headings for monographs have not been well developed by Library of Congress catalogers so that subject access has been weak; foreign materials are often difficult to acquire, and, if acquired, may not be cataloged; and most of the literature appears in journals and newsletters. Also, most of the literature is available in a single language, and is thus unavailable to those who cannot read that language. Indexing and abstracting services pick up only some articles; for example, it is the policy of some services *not* to index items from newsletters. Yet, as chapters 2 and 6 pointed out, newsletters have played a crucial role in the development of the preservation and conservation fields.

According to Smith, the invisible college—a useful source of information within countries—is not yet well developed in the international preservation community. She feels that this is because the international preservation information system is relatively new. In many parts of the world, there is not yet a critical mass of preservation colleagues ("Dissemination . . . ," p. 247). And in many places there is no easy way to communicate, since telephones might not even be available. An invisible college and the distribution of gray literature depend on cohorts--people who can be spoken to or whom one can discuss issues with face to face.

Informal communication through invisible colleges has been most successful in countries or regions where one can easily and inexpensively makes phone calls or run into colleagues at programs or conferences. These informal channels work less well between countries where the problems of time zone differences, language barriers, the expense of phone calls, or the lack of high-tech equipment, and so on, impede such means of communication. The rise in the use of electronic mail greatly facilitates and increases communication across borders. Yet such communication depends on computers, and the whole world is not yet plugged in.

Ellen McCrady has already begun a grass-roots effort to disseminate conservation and preservation information widely via her editorship and authorship of the *Abbey Newsletter*. Several years ago she began mailing out complimentary subscriptions to her contacts at libraries or archives in countries where currency problems kept them from subscribing to the *Newsletter*. Over time she learned that the *Newsletters* were not necessarily getting disseminated. Now she will not send complimentary subscriptions unless the recipients can demonstrate that they are sharing them (Interview with McCrady, 2/22/93). In the most recent issue of the *Newsletter* (17.5, October 1993, 65-66), McCrady announced an adoption program whereby readers may adopt subscribers from other countries by paying for their subscriptions. Readers may adopt subscribers anonymously, or be introduced by McCrady. She hopes that "some pen pal correspondence may develop as a result" of the program.

As I have suggested, the dissemination of published preservation information is also hampered throughout the world because of language barriers. There are few multilingual sources, and few items are translated. The Commission on Preservation and Access has translated some of its publications as well as *Slow Fires: On the Preservation of the Human Record*, video and film versions of which were produced in the United States in 1988 (see bibliography). Also, many Canadian publications are available in both French and English. The pros and cons of machine translation for the vast majority of items that are not yet translated will be discussed below.

Could new technologies help erase geographical boundaries and ultimately lead to an electronically-based cohort where colleagues could share documents and communicate regularly with one another? Unlike the traditional cohort, "electronic cohorts" need never meet one another except over the network. This is certainly feasible from a technological standpoint, but it still excludes people who live in parts of the world where the technology is not yet available. Still, the technologies described below have the potential to aid in the dissemination of preservation information. The benefits of electronic communication may trickle down. News now travels rapidly and more people than ever before can receive it simultaneously. Therefore, theoretically everyone receives information more quickly than in the past because word of mouth spreads the information which has been conveyed via television and computers. Small distribution centers could be established in places where the technology exists. The resulting links could be the basis of additional distribution and communication.

New technologies can do much more than distribute publications, however. Although past preservation education efforts have focused on bringing the student to the institution, the institution can now be brought to the student. This can be done via electronic or satellite channels, as described below.

As I will consider below, three methods of disseminating information, electronic (using a computer over the Internet), distance learning via satellite, and machine translation (which uses local computers), can be used to enhance education. The goal here is not to describe specific systems—which will soon be replaced by newer technologies anyway—but to discuss their potential use in the dissemination of preservation information and the development of new educational models.

Electronic Communication

It has been said that the computer, even more than the printing press or any other technological tool, has increased the world's use of paper. For example, we all know the effect that computerized mailing lists have had on the volume of junk mail which we now receive. Many of us are producing more paper drafts of our work than ever before because it is easy to push that *print* key. An increasing amount of information is now being created and distributed—and not just on paper. Those of us who work in institutions with good telecommunication capabilities have electronic and voice mail to contend with in addition to paper mail.

The avalanche of information which confronts us via multiple channels is impossible to assimilate. [Perhaps the second most useful key on the computer after *print* is *delete*.] But what about voice mail, cellular phones, satellite dishes bringing in over 100 television stations from all over the world, talking wrist-watches, and portable computers? Information is constantly assailing us from everywhere. There is much more information around us than we have time for, and soon we may be forced to create "information-free" zones just to get away from it all. With all of this noise in the universe, how can we best communicate with one another?

Technology is not inherently chaotic; rather it is sometimes conceived, designed, and used poorly. The Internet exemplifies the best and worst aspects of electronic technologies: it contains vast amounts of information, but it is so poorly organized that it is cumbersome to use, providing the user with high recall but low precision.

With electronic technologies one can disseminate information in a timely manner. So electronic publishing is ideal for bibliographies or other information, such as a list of disaster-recovery suppliers and consultants, which needs to be augmented, corrected, or updated frequently. The information can be used at the terminal or printed or stored for later use. Gradually, an increasing number of scholarly journals are also being produced and published electronically. Submission, editing, and publication all occur online, so the lag time between authorship, manuscript submission, and publication is greatly reduced.

Library school instruction is also offered online. At Punjabi University in India, for example, one can obtain a library degree through distance learning. This idea has its roots in correspondence courses. Now classes are run through e-mail, satellite hookups (see below), and Internet as well as through personal contact courses. In England, Loughborough University's Computers in Teaching Initiative (CTI) Center, funded by the Higher Education Funding Council, is developing computer distance learning programs. (Information about both Loughborough and Punjabi was provided by Jagtar Singh in my interview with him on 3/15/93.)

Computer learning can also supplement classroom instruction. Electronic mail forums continue discussions started in class. And interactive media have been used in schools for several years now; students can move through modules at their own pace. One university in the United States has applied for funding to create a computer-based preservation-training course for librarians across the U.S. The courses would be produced in multiple formats using both Macintosh and MS-DOS platforms. If successful in the U.S., the courses could be offered to other countries (confidential interview).

Electronic communication also makes it possible to distribute preservation information quickly, and to many people at the same time. Through the Conservation Distribution List (CONSDIST.LIST), for example, which is supported by Stanford University and managed by Walter Henry, one may submit questions for posting to the list. Responses to queries are posted about twice a week; emergency responses are even more expeditious. Information posted covers both the conservation and preservation fields. The CONSDIST.LIST is also an excellent forum for sending announcements, job advertisements, or information about new treatments, supplies, suppliers, technologies, or other useful data.

Conservation Online (CoOL), a Wide Area Information Server (WAIS), provides Internet access to a full-text database of conservation publications of interest to librarians, archivists, and curators. It was also developed at Stanford University.

Distance Education (DE) via Satellite

A number of library schools have held classes off campus in sites remote from the central campus in order to facilitate part-time or distance students. Some universities have also had continuing education mandates. Now many universities are getting away from traditional methods of continuing and part-time off-campus programs because they are so labor intensive and time consuming—particularly when faculty members have to drive great distances. With satellite hook-ups students in remote locations can participate in classes on campus. Faculty need to make only occasional site visits.

Several universities in the United States have successful satellite distance education (DE) programs, and one of them, the University of Hawaii, will soon be offering courses to students in the Pacific Rim. Language barriers can be overcome by using simultaneous translators, as well as by having the courses taught by multilingual instructors.

The technologies in use vary from campus to campus; some have one-way video with two-way audio teleconferencing; some use open-circuit television; some use cable television companies to deliver courses nationally. Some have courses taped and beamed to another site, where a local instructor plays the tapes and answers question on site. Panelists representing several of the campuses with distance learning programs described them at the Association of Library and Information Science Education (ALISE) meeting in Denver at a session on January 21, 1993.

For a paper on distance learning for preservation, Teresa Lupe Grenot, one of my students, interviewed two professors in February 1993: Roger Wyatt (Emporia State University), and Daniel Barron (University of South Carolina) (unpublished student paper written in March 1993 for GSLIS 486, "Issues and Problems in Preservation"). Although neither school was at that time offering preservation courses as part of their distance learning programs, Wyatt and Barron saw the potential. Both felt, however, that in areas requiring hands-on experience, the satellite approach alone would not be sufficient. The use of adjunct faculty to supplement the distance learning part of the course was a possibility suggested by Barron (Grenot, pp. 7-10).

The potential of satellite courses for international preservation education is worth investigating. The success of library science distance education programs in the United States alone suggests that the potential to adapt such programs to the preservation field exists. Some work has already been undertaken to develop international information science programs using electronic networks. Syracuse University undertook a feasibility study for UNESCO. The participating countries were Brazil, China, Ethiopia, Kenya, Malaysia, Mexico, Morocco, Nigeria, the Philippines, and Venezuela (Dosa and Katzer, "Electronic Networking"). The Syracuse project resulted in a new concept: Distance Technical Assistance (DTA). This concept is slightly different than that of distance education; DTA connects colleagues with one another while DE usually connects student and teacher. The electronic networking program has been supported by the International Federation for Information and Documentation (FID), UNESCO, and the United States government.

Dosa and Katzer feel that the impact of transnational networking, once regularized, will be profound because ". . . the creativity, talent, and ideas at work in developing countries represent the capital of the future" (95). Although Dosa and Katzer used an electronic network for their study—which lent itself well to the one-to-one concept of DTA—the application of satellite hook ups to link classrooms worldwide seems worthy of investigation.

The American library schools, state departments of education, and state library agencies which offer distance learning programs organized the Library and Information Science Distance Education Consortium (LISDEC) in 1990. This organization gathers and disseminates information on distance learning programs.

Since these programs and organizations for library and information science distance education are already in place, the international preservation community should build on these resources to study the feasibility of developing its own such courses. From writings on the subject we have an idea of the elements necessary for a successful program: satellite access, high-production-value video material, the inclusion of prominent figures as presenters in the courses, designated site coordinators or facilitators, supplemental materials, and interactive elements via telephones, fax machines, and electronic mail (Barron, "The Use and Perceived Barriers," and Barron, "Perceptions of Faculty and Administrative Staff").

Translation and Machine Translation (MT)

Merrily Smith discusses weaknesses of the preservation information system as it now exists: materials are scattered throughout the world, libraries do not acquire all the material that is available, foreign materials are not always cataloged, and there is an absence of preservation bibliographies and comprehensive multi-lingual glossaries and dictionaries (Smith, "Dissemination," 244-245). The problem of scattered literature could be mitigated by making publications available online. Then professionals would not have to wait until they were cataloged, and the publications could be sent around the world on demand. In some libraries, foreign materials are given a low priority for cataloging. By translating documents and making them available online as well as on paper, they will be more accessible.

Translations, however, are time-consuming and therefore expensive to prepare. In order to translate specialized documents, the translator must have not only language and writing skills, but also a working knowledge of the terminology of the field. Yet, even within a language, terms are not used with consistency. For example until about ten years ago, the terms *conservation* and *preservation* were used interchangeably in the U.S. The terms *alkaline*, *acid-free*, and *archival* are sometimes wrongly used to mean the same thing. There needs to be a controlled vocabulary for the field.

The process of translation could be facilitated if such a vocabulary in a multi-lingual glossary or thesaurus was prepared which included terms for the conservation and preservation fields. This is not any easy undertaking, but it could be organized through IFLA's PAC Core Programme. (The International Council on Archives (ICA) published the *Glossary of Basic Archival and Library Conservation Terms* in 1988 with terms in English, Spanish, German, Italian, French, and Russian.) Although such reference tools are not a prerequisite for preparing translations, they would provide standardization of terms, assuring that translations would be more consistent.

Translations can be done manually or through the use of computers. This latter method is known as machine translation or MT. Machine translators have been in existence since the early 1930s; and the Electronic Numerical Integrator and Calculator (ENIAC) was developed in 1946 (Vasconcellos, "Machine Translation," 153).

Over the past ten years MT has become more sophisticated. There are now three basic computerized systems: direct translations, syntactical transfer, and interlingual (Hovy, "How MT Works"). The simplest (and therefore the most primitive) forms are the direct translation systems. These systems merely encode dictionaries, phrases, and words. The result is a translation in a rather stilted language which might be serviceable, but certainly not elegant. The direct systems may not capture the inherent ambiguities of languages. For example, the computer might not understand the multiple meanings of words in the sentence, "the limping car turned into the driveway." To the computer, "turned into" could mean "became" or it could refer to the physical movement of the car. The advantages of direct systems are that their programs are available on personal computers, and that they work for basic documents.

Syntactical transfer systems encode information into grammars, lexicons, and transfer rules. The computer actually parses each sentence, so that once it is translated into another language the translation is more natural than in the direct systems. These systems are complex, relying on more computer memory. However the literature on the subject that I have seen does not consider how this or the other systems work beyond the sentence level. A computer translation may be able to translate "I have two calves" into another language. Out of context, the translation may convert "calves" into either small cows or leg muscles. In context, the conversion may be more accurate.

Interlingual systems translate text using a central data-representation notation called an *interlingua*. These systems are built on a set of transfer rules. This is the most tedious system of all to build as it relies on deep semantic representations. These systems are still in the developmental stage at several universities including Carnegie Mellon and New Mexico State University (Hovy, 172).

Eduard Hovy predicts that in the future all major MT systems will be hybrids (176). Some of the more sophisticated direct systems have already evolved into syntactical transfer systems. But all of these still require refinement. None of them can as yet measure up to skillful human translations.

The demand for MT has never been greater, however. The Canadian government, the EC, and other political bodies need to have reams of documents translated yearly. There are professional organizations for people working in machine translation including the International Association for Machine Translation (IAMT); MT is definitely a growth industry. And there is at least one inherent advantage to MT: human translators necessarily bring their own biases (however subtle) to their work. MT removes the bias. If MT can be perfected, it may produce better translations than people can, or at least produce acceptable ones much more quickly than human beings can.

An additional issue is that MT will cost money to develop and then to apply to conservation and preservation texts. At very least, someone must be paid to identify important works to be translated and to see to it that the conversion is done. (See chapter 5 for funding issues.)

For basic-level documents that are procedural rather than highly theoretical, direct systems may be sufficient--for example, emergency procedures, lists of disaster-recovery suppliers and consultants, conservation supply catalogs, etc. Translations for this type of document would be easy to produce. Furthermore, MT can reduce the time and money required for the bulk translation of repetitive documents, such as government publications, which are often reissued year after year with only minor changes.

For documents with more complicated text, human translation is still the most effective method. For the next several years, at least, the preservation field should focus its efforts on producing multilingual thesauri and glossaries and then on identifying key documents to translate.

There is another impediment to international communication online worth mentioning here: formatting. For example, my electronic mail system does not have multiple character sets; it does not even have diacritics. There are software programs available for personal computers which contain fonts for dozens of languages, however. But the point here is that even if one has fluency in other languages, she might not have at her disposal the necessary character sets for communicating easily and accurately. The mechanisms for written international communication need fine tuning.

If Not Now, When?

Though the technologies described above are advancing daily, they are not yet fully integrated everywhere; it may be a long time before developing countries have the capabilities to participate fully online (though they will benefit indirectly with the wider dissemination of information). Besides the issue of universal availability of information, there are still many other challenges ahead. Some of these are discussed by Ben Davis in "Looking and Learning Through Computers"; for example: international standards in computing, telecommunications, and media types; the resolution of a host of copyright problems; and "the complexity of factors associated with the synchronization and distribution of an ever-increasing and converging variety of media technologies. . . " (22).

The preservation and conservation fields have already begun to take advantage of new technologies. The invisible colleges in the U.S. and Canada are exchanging information on the Conservation Distribution List; soon we will have an international preser/conservation distribution list.

The cultural and technological environment of the 1990s should make the gathering and disseminating of information worldwide increasingly easier. The potential for preservation education is enormous.

8. What IFLA Can Do

IFLA has played a significant role in advancing conservation and preservation in libraries and archives around the world through the PAC Core Programme and the Section on Conservation. The following recommendations, organized under the categories established in chapter 1, are addressed to both the Section and the Core Programme. Some of the recommendations fit into the goals of the 1992-1997 Medium-Term Programme, as articulated by Merrily Smith at the Moscow 1991 IFLA Conference.[1] Others might not be feasible for the PAC Core until the next Medium-Term Programme. After each recommendation there appears one or more of the following designations: "Section," "Core-Programme, 1992-97," or "Core-Programme Beyond 1997," as appropriate.

A. *Collaboration*

1) **Using IFLA's collaborations with UNESCO and ICA as models, develop educational initiatives with other organizations such as the Commission on Preservation and Access, the Getty Conservation Institute, and regional groups such as the European Confederation of Conservator-Restorers' Organizations and the Association for the Conservation of the Cultural Patrimony of the Americas** (Core-Programme Beyond 1997).

B. *Educational Activities*

2) **Promote educational opportunities in library schools. These include the integration of preservation topics in core curricula and courses in preservation for library school students, and continuing education courses for practicing librarians** (Core-Programme, 1992-97).

3) **Consider incorporating library schools into the programs of the 5 PAC Regional Centres. The library schools could work with the Regional Center Libraries to co-sponsor educational programs** (Core-Programme Beyond 1997).

4) **Establish a forum for teachers of preservation** (Core-Programme, 1992-1997).

5) **Convene another international education conference as a follow-up to that in 1986 in Vienna titled "Education and Training for Preservation and Conservation"** (Core-Programme, 1992-97).

---

[1] These are: 1) raise conservation and preservation consciousness; 2) disseminate information; 3) prepare educational materials for dissemination; 4) promote education and training; and, 5) continue research and cooperative programmes.

C. *Dissemination of Preservation Information*

6) **Publish the *International Preservation Newsletter* more regularly** (Core-Programme, 1992-97).

7) **Publish a preservation column in the *IFLA Journal* in addition to the annual PAC report. There could be guest columnists from different institutions around the world** (Section).

8) **Distribute publications through the PAC Regional Centres** (Core-Programme, 1992-97).

9) **Work with UNESCO and ICA to find a more effective way to disseminate the RAMP studies. Explore electronic publishing of them on Internet as well as wider distribution of paper copies for countries without access to Internet** (Core-Programme, 1992-97).

10) **Compile a multi-lingual glossary of preservation and conservation terms as an aid to translations and to establish a consistent vocabulary. Examine the IFLA Art Section and the ICA multi-lingual glossaries for models** (Section).

11) **Promote the cross-fertilization of ideas through electronic information exchange** (Section).

12) **Offer a program or programs at the IFLA annual conferences on some of the new technologies described in chapter 7 such as electronic networks, distance learning for preservation, and so on** (Section).

D. *Resources and Funding*

13) **Explore funding opportunities to enhance the IFLA/PAC goals. Potential areas for funding include internships (Mellon, Getty Conservation Institute, Commission on Preservation and Access); publications (the European Commission on Preservation and Access); and research (Volkswagen Foundation; corporations)** (Core-Programme Beyond 1997).

E. *General Strategies*

14) **The fortunes of preservation are closely tied to the fortunes of libraries. In order for preservation specialists to play an active role in determining library priorities, they must learn a good deal more about management. IFLA can help these specialists accomplish this by stressing management issues in their training programs** (Core-Programme, 1992-97).

15) **Sustain current levels of activity even in light of shrinking monetary resources; seek new sources for support, especially among private corporations. In financially stringent times, governments are not as likely to fund library activities, though there is currently a window of opportunity in Europe through the Commission of the European Communities** (Section; Core-Programme, 1992-97).

16) **Preservation of *all* cultures needs to be prioritized** (Section; Core-Programme, 1992-97; Core-Programme Beyond 1997).

F. *Regional Conservation Treatment Centers*

17) **Explore the establishment of regional conservation treatment centers, possibly in coordination with the PAC Regional Centres. Alexander Wilson, in his 1988 report, *Library Policy for Preservation . . .*, recommended that the Commission of the European Communities consider the feasibility of regional centers in Europe (recommendation 20, p. 140). Such centers would provide physical treatment services, disaster recovery assistance, general information, and internship opportunities** (Core-Programme Beyond 1997).

G. *Research*

18) **Promote research not only in conservation laboratories, but in schools of library and information science** (Core-Programme Beyond 1997).

19) **Continue to promote collaborative research projects with other organizations. (Once the European Commission on Preservation and Access is established, there may be opportunities to coordinate joint research projects among IFLA Regional Centres, universities, and corporations.)** (Core-Programme, 1992-97).

9. Conclusion

> Scientific communication is perhaps the most important tangible tool for doing science. Through default, ignorance, and lack of concern, the worldwide scientific communication system has evolved in such a way that it maximally benefits those countries and communities which are already highly developed in science and handicaps those which are less developed and need it most.
>
> There are good reasons for the prominent role of communication in scientific activities. Research in the natural sciences is, . . . a highly collective undertaking. Scientists learn from the work of others and build on it.
>
> It is now known that one of the crucial modules of scientific research is the 'invisible college' . . . (geographically spread over the world) . . . [which has] a vital influence on the direction of research in a given area . . . . If the scientific manpower of a given country is outside such 'invisible colleges,' the country is likely to be forced to resign itself to mediocrity." (Moravcsik, *Science Development*, 69-70).

The word *science* in this quotation could easily be replaced with either *conservation* or *preservation*. Communication and collaboration have been crucial to the development of the conservation and preservation fields. An early, yet still striking, example of international collaboration came in 1966 after the flood in Florence. Conservators and librarians converged in Italy and exchanged ideas thus developing new methods for the salvage of flood-damaged materials.

Yet as the quotation stresses, some countries are left out of the communication loop in international preservation planning. If we overemphasize the use of new communication technologies, such countries may be left even further behind. A more optimistic way to view the effectiveness of new technologies sees information as traveling with increasing speed to countries that have electronic access, and therefore ultimately reaching all places faster. But that may not in fact happen. International professional associations have a responsibility to disseminate information in a variety of ways. For the foreseeable future, preservation information should be distributed as widely as possible through electronic and paper means.

** *** ** *** **

This report has looked at the historical background, current practices, and possible opportunities of preservation education. Strengths and weaknesses of the current political and economic climate have also been discussed--for example, the retrenchment of preservation and conservation programs in universities and the closure of library schools in the U.S.

Despite the pessimism which I expressed about library schools in the preface and in chapter 1, I remain convinced that they are important places for preservation education. Only universities can offer both degree programs and opportunities to carry out research. However, aspects of preservation education are also well provided for in other settings such as libraries, archives, regional conservation centers, and networks. For library schools to thrive, and the preservation field to continue to grow, all of these institutions must support one another. One way to foster mutual support is through joint sponsorship of continuing education programs.

Preservation education will expand through the 1990s in a variety of institutions and through numerous communication channels. Never before have the opportunities for the dissemination of information been greater.

Appendix A

INTERVIEWEES

S.K. Agyei
Department of Library and Archival Studies
University of Ghana

Patricia Battin
Commission on Preservation and Access
Washington, D.C.

Lourdes Blanco
Centro Nacional de Conservación Documental
Biblioteca Nacional de Venezuela

Sally Buchanan
School of Library and Information Science
University of Pittsburgh

Terry Cannon
Research and Development Department
British Library

Margaret Child
Preservation Consultant
Washington, D.C.

David Clements
British Library

Donald Davis
Graduate School of Library and Information Science
University of Texas at Austin

John Day
University of Northumbria

Mohammed Jamin Lebai Din
National Archives of Malaysia

Richard Ekman
Andrew W. Mellon Foundation
New York City

Josephine Fang
Graduate School of Library and Information Science
Simmons College
Boston, Massachusetts

George Farr
Division of Preservation and Access
National Endowment for the Humanities
Washington, D.C.

John Feather
Department of Library and Information Studies
Loughborough University of Technology

Mirjam M. Foot
British Library

Maria Lilli di Franco
Istituto Centrale per la Patologia del Libro
Rome

Sharlane T. Grant
Arizona State University Libraries

Carolyn Harris
Graduate School of Library and Information Science
University of Texas at Austin

Gladys Jusu-Sheriff
Institute of Library and Information Studies
University of Sierra Leone

Michael Koenig
Graduate School of Library and Information Science
Rosary College
River Forest, Illinois

Gabriela Krist
International Centre for the Study of Preservation and the Restoration of Cultural Property (ICCROM)
Rome

Michael Lesk
Bellcore
Morristown, New Jersey

Jan Lyall
National Library of Australia

Ellen McCrady
Abbey Publications
Austin, Texas

J.H. McIlwaine
School of Library Studies
University College London

John McIntyre
National Library of Scotland, Edinburgh

Cheryl Metoyer-Duran
Graduate School of Library and Information Science, University of California, Los Angeles
and
Rupert Costo Chair in American Indian History, University of California, Riverside

Sherelyn Ogden
Northeast Document Conservation Center
Andover, Massachusetts

Antonio Papa
Centro di Fotoriproduzione Legatoria e Restauro degli Archivi di Stato
Rome

Hans Peder Pedersen
Det Kongelige Danske Kunstakademi Konservatorskolen
Copenhagen

Frank D. Preusser, Consultant
(formerly of the Getty Conservation Institute)
Marina del Rey, California

Ann Russell
Northeast Document Conservation Center
Andover, Massachusetts

Hans Rütimann
Commission on Preservation and Access
Washington, D.C.

Jagtar Singh
Department of Library and Information Science
Punjabi University
Patiala, India

Merrily A. Smith
Library of Congress
Washington, D.C.

Susan G. Swartzburg
Rutgers, The State University of New Jersey
New Brunswick, New Jersey

Marta de la Torre
Getty Conservation Institute
Marina del Rey, California

Karen Turko
University of Toronto Library

John R. Turner
Department of Information and Library Studies
University of Wales

P.E. Westra
South African Library

Paul Wilson
School of Information, Library and Archive Studies
University of New South Wales

A.J. Wood
Faculty of Community Studies and Education
Manchester Metropolitan University

Appendix B

QUESTIONNAIRES

Questionnaire 1: Educators

1. Do you teach a course in preservation or conservation? (If not, please skip to question #4)

2. If yes, name the course and briefly describe its content.

3. Please also describe your approach (e.g., practical, theoretical, lecture, seminar, etc.)

4. Do you teach any courses which contain a preservation or conservation component? (For example, archives)

5. If yes, name each course and briefly describe the content of each one.

6. How does preservation/conservation fit into the overall curriculum of your school?

7. Are there courses in other departments in your university which relate to preservation or conservation? (e.g., chemistry, engineering, anthropology, archaeology, art, art history, film studies, architecture, etc.)

8. If so, name them. Are these courses either recommended or required?

9. Are there internship programs in your area?

10. Does your institution offer continuing education courses in preservation or conservation?

11. If so, please list and describe them.

12. Do you address cultural diversity issues in your courses? (e.g., the nature and variety of records in diverse cultural settings; whether the records of these groups are being preserved and how they are being preserved)

13. Are you an adjunct faculty member or do you teach full time?

14. What is the highest degree that you have earned?

15. Where did you receive your preservation or conservation training?

16. Please describe preservation activities in your country (organizations, etc.).

Questionnaire 2: Practitioners/Researchers

1. Briefly describe your duties and responsibilities.

2. If you were not originally trained in conservation or preservation (e.g., if you are a chemist, automation expert, etc.), how and why did you become connected with these fields?

3. What do you see as the critical issues for conservation and preservation in the 1990s? What steps should be taken to address these issues?

4. Identify some international issues that the field must address.

5. If you are a researcher, please describe your current projects.

6. Do you teach courses or workshops in conservation or preservation? (Please list classes taught)

   If so, are you affiliated with a particular institution or program?

7. Do you take on interns or apprentices? If so, briefly describe your training program.

8. Where did you receive your training?

9. Please describe any other programs of interest in your region or country.

Questionnaire 3: Consultants and Funding Agencies

1. Briefly describe your duties and responsibilities.

2. If you were not originally trained in conservation or preservation (e.g., if you are a chemist, automation expert, etc.), how and why did you become connected with these fields?

3. What do you see as the critical issues for conservation and preservation in the 1990s? What steps should be taken to address these issues?

4. Identify some international issues that the field must address.

5. What are some of the projects you or your organization are currently funding? What are some of the projects accepted but not yet funded?

6. What are some of the difficulties in obtaining funding? What projects are the easiest to fund? the most difficult? How do you set funding priorities?

7. Is preservation a separate department in your organization, or is it handled by general administration?

8. Does your organization hire people previously trained in preservation or do you train them with the necessary skills to carry out their jobs?

Table A: Existing Sources for Preservation Education

Library Schools

modules within core courses
preservation and conservation courses
certificate programs

Professional Associations

seminars
workshops
programs at meetings/conferences
publications (including all media)

Regional Conservation Centers (U.S.)

workshops
consultants
publications
internships at centers

Regional Networks

workshops
consultants
publications

Large Libraries and Archives

may train personnel from other libraries
internships

National Libraries and Archives

workshops
publications
internships

Table B: Emerging Sources for Preservation Education

Political Entities
(e.g., the European Community)

Networks
(esp. electronic)

Collaborative Efforts of Library Schools
(e.g., Preservation Intensive Institute, U.S.)

Collaborative Efforts of Library Schools and Libraries
(e.g., through distance learning initiatives)

Table C: Methods of Disseminating Preservation Information

Workshops, courses, seminars, conference programs

Consultants

Publications

Internships

Information exchange at meetings

Informal communication
(e.g., the 'invisible college'--meetings, phone calls, letters, electronic mail)

Teleconferencing

Interactive video

Distance learning

television (satellite)
electronic networks
computer-assisted instruction

Table D: Elements of Current Preservation Curricula

The Context of Conservation and Preservation

Organization and Planning of Preservation Programs
- needs and priorities
- condition surveys
- preservation policy
- environmental issues
- staff and user training
- disaster preparedness
- mass treatments

Management of Preservation Activities
- collection management
- selection for preservation
- minor mending and repair
- library binding and contracting for services
- conservation treatment
- reformatting
- new technologies
- budgeting and fund raising
- cooperative, national, and international programs
- consciousness-raising about preservation (local, national, and international)

Protection and Care of Library Materials
- environmental enemies (biological agents and temperature and relative humidity)
- protective storage methods
- care in use
- transportation
- copying
- exhibition
- building planning
- fumigation techniques
- cleaning of storage areas
- flattening paper
- deciphering faded documents

Other

cultural diversity and the concept of cultural heritage
ethical issues

(Sources: C. Harris, Univ. of Texas/GSLIS; Y.P. Kathpalia, UNESCO Ramp Study, PGI-84/WS/2, *A Model Curriculum* . . .; M.A. Smith, "Preservation Education in Library Schools," in J.R. Fang and A. Russell, *Education Training for Preservation and Conservation*, IFLA Pub. 54; M.V. Cloonan, UCLA/GSLIS; D.W.G. Clements, "Preservation and Library School Education . . . .")

BIBLIOGRAPHY

Abbey Newsletter, vol. 1, no 1, 1975-.

Abbott, Andrew. *The System of Professions: An Essay on the Division of Expert Labor.* Chicago: University of Chicago Press, 1988.

Abt, Jeffrey. "Objectifying the Book: The Impact of Science on Books and Manuscripts." *Library Trends* 36.1 (Summer 1987): 23-38.

American Institute for Conservation of Historic and Artistic Works. *Directory, 1984-85*. Washington, D.C.: AIC, 1984.

---. *Directory, 1994*. Washington, D.C.: 1993.

---. *The Book and Paper Group Annual*. v. 11. Washington, D.C.: AIC, 1992.

American Library Association. *ALA Handbook of Organization, 1992-93*. Chicago: American Library Association, 1992.

Anderson, Michael. "The Preservation of Machine-Readable Data for Secondary Analysis." *Archives* 17.74 (October 1985): 79-93.

Andrew W. Mellon Foundation. *Report from January 1, 1991 through December 31, 1991*. New York: Andrew W. Mellon Foundation, [1992].

Arnoult, Jean-Marie. "Annual Report 1991-1992 of the PAC Core Programme." *IFLA Journal* 19.2 (1993): 213-223.

Association of Research Libraries. *Preservation Statistics, 1990-91*. Washington, D.C.: ARL, 1992.

---. *Report of the Association of Research Libraries Working Group on the Review of the NEH Preservation Program.* Washington, D.C.: ARL, May 1993. Unpublished Report.

---. Preservation Planning Program. [Resource Guides]. Washington, D.C.: ARL, 1993.
Organizing Preservation Activities (Michèle Cloonan)
Options for Replacing and Reformatting Deteriorated Materials (Jennifer Banks)
Collections Conservation (Robert DeCandido)
Managing a Library Binding Program (Jan Merrill-Oldham)
Collection Maintenance and Improvement (Sherry Byrne)
Disaster Preparedness (Constance Brooks)

Staff Training and User Awareness in Preservation Management (Wesley L. Boomgaarden)

Atkins, Winston, and Ellen Belcher. "Coordinating a Bomb Blast Recovery." *Conservation Administration News* 55 (October 1993): 1-2, 24, 25-27.

Badu, Edwin Ellis. "The Preservation of Library Materials: A Case Study of University of Science and Technology Library in Ghana." *Aslib Proceedings* 42.4 (April 1990): 119-125.

Banks, Paul N. "Education for Conservators." *Library Journal* 104.8 (May 1, 1979): 1013-17.

Barron, Daniel L. "Perceptions of Faculty and Administrative Staff in ALA-Accredited Programs toward Part-Time and Distance Students in LIS Education." *Journal of Education for Library and Information Science* 34.3 (Summer 1993): 187-199.

---. "The Use and Perceived Barriers to Use of Telecommunications Technology." *Journal of Education for Library and Information Science* 27.4 (Spring 1987): 288-294.

Battin, Patricia. "'As Far Into the Future As Possible': Choice and Cooperation in the 1990s." In *Advances in Preservation and Access*, ed. by Barbra Buckner Higginbotham and Mary E. Jackson, 41-48. Westport, Conn.: Meckler, 1992.

Berry, John, and Judy Quinn. "Consensus Out of Chaos." *Library Journal* 116.13 (August 1991): 42-46.

Books in Peril: Symposium on the Preservation of Library and Archival Materials in Southern Africa. Cape Town, South Africa: South African Library, 1987. (Proceedings from a symposium held at the South African Library, Cape Town, November 19-21, 1986.)

Buchanan, Sally A. "The Third Decade: Directions for Preservation [and] Conservation." *Conservation Administration News* 33 (April 1988): 3, 10.

Chepesiuk, Ron. "The Dawn of European Economic Unity: What it Means for Libraries." *American Libraries* 23.3 (March 1992): 212-215.

---. "Information Policy as Cultural Policy: A Conference for a New Europe." *American Libraries* 24.2 (February 1993): 162, 164.

Child, Margaret S. *Directory of Information Sources on Scientific Research Related to the Preservation of Sound Recordings, Still and Moving Images and Magnetic Tape.* Washington, D.C.: The Commission on Preservation and Access, September 1993.

Clareson, Tom, et al. "Nationwide Preservation Survey Looks at Management, Filming, Environmental Controls." (Special Report) *Commission on Preservation and Access Newsletter* 39 (October 1991): 3-4.

Clements, David W.G. "Preservation and Library School Education Programmes." *Library Association Record* 88.3 (March 1986): 136-37.

---, et al. *Review of Training Needs in Preservation and Conservation.* (PGI-89/WS/15) Paris: Unesco, 1989.

Cloonan, Michèle Valerie. "Mass Deacidification in the 1990s." *Rare Books & Manuscripts Librarianship* 5.2 (1990): 95-103.

---. *Organizing Preservation Activities*. (Preservation Planning Program, Resource Guide) Washington, D.C.: Association of Research Libraries, 1993.

---. "The Preservation of Knowledge." *Library Trends* 41.4 (Spring 1993): 594-604.

---, et al. "Preservation Education in American Library Schools: Recounting the Ways." *Journal of Education for Library and Information Science* 31.3 (Winter 1991): 187-203.

---, and Patricia C. Norcott. "Evolution of Preservation Librarianship as Reflected in Job Descriptions from 1975 through 1987." *College & Research Libraries* 50.6 (November 1989): 646-656.

Commission on Preservation and Access. *Annual Report, July 1, 1991 - June 30, 1992.* Washington, D.C.: The Commission on Preservation and Access, [1992].

---. *Annual Report, July 1, 1992 - June 30, 1993*. Washington, D.C.: The Commission on Preservation and Access, [1993].

---. Review and Assessment Committee. *Final Report, September 26, 1991.* Washington, D.C.: Commission on Preservation and Access, [1991].

Conservation Administration News. No. 1, June 1979.

Conservation Distribution List. "Storage of Color Photographic Materials." October 21, 1993. (Electronic mail dist. list.)

Conway, Paul. "Archival Preservation: Definitions for Improving Education and Training." *Restaurator* 10.2 (1989): 47-60.

Cowell, Alan. "Bomb Outside Uffizi in Florence Kills 6 and Damages Many Works." *New York Times,* May 28, 1993, A1, A8.

---. "Bombing in Florence: 'Hidden Hand'?" *New York Times*, June 3, 1993, A7.

---. "Uffizi Reopens 24 Days After Bombing." *New York Times,* June 21, 1993, B1, B4.

Crowe, William J. "Verner W. Clapp as Opinion Leader and Change Agent in the Preservation of Library Materials." Ph.D. diss., Indiana University, 1986.

Cunha, George Martin. "Mass Deacidification for Libraries. *Library Technology Reprts* 23.3 (May-June 1987): 361-472.

---. "Mass Deacidification for Libraries: 1989 Update." *Library Technology Reports* 25.1 (January-February): 11-81.

Darling, Pamela. "Creativity v. Despair: The Challenge of Preservation Administration." *Library Trends* 30.2 (Fall 1981): 179-88.

---. "To the Editor." *Conservation Administration News* 22 (July 1985): 3, 20.

---, and Sherelyn Ogden. "From Problems Perceived to Programs in Practice: The Preservation of Library Resources in the U.S.A., 1956-1980." *Library Resources & Technical Services* 25.1 (January-March 1981): 9-29.

---, et al. *Preservation Planning Program: An Assisted Self-Study Manual for Libraries.* Expanded ed. Washington, D.C.: Association of Research Libraries, Office of Management Services, 1987.

Davis, Ben. "Looking and Learning Through Computers." *EDUCOM Review* 28.1 (January/February 1993): 20-25.

DePew, John N. *A Library Media and Archival Preservation Handbook.* Santa Barbara, Ca.: ABC/Clio, 1991.

DeWhitt, Benjamin L. "Long-Term Preservation of Data on Computer Magnetic Media: Part I." *Conservation Administration News* 29 (April 1987): 7, 19, 28.

---. "Long-Term Preservation of Data on Computer Magnetic Media: Part II." *Conservation Administration News* 30 (July 1987): 4, 24.

Dorn, Knut. *Champagne Taste and a Beer Budget: The Problem of Increasing Scholarly Publishing in Europe and Decreasing Academic Library Budgets in North America.* Paper presented at the annual meeting of the Center for Research Libraries, Chicago, April 24, 1992. Offprint.

Dornberg, John. "Germany: Pride and Patronage." *ARTnews* 91.8 (October 1992): 100-101.

Dosa, Marta and Jeffrey Katzer. "Electronic Networking in Support of South-to-South Cooperation." *Journal of Education for Library and Information Science* 32.1-2 (Summer/Fall 1991): 84-96.

Dougherty, Richard M., and Carol Hughes. *Preferred Futures for Libraries: A Summary of Six Workshops with University Provosts and Library Directors*. Mountain View, CA: The Research Libraries Group, 1991.

---. *Preferred Library Futures II: Charting the Paths*. Mountain View, CA: The Research Libraries Group, 1993.

Elkington, Nancy, ed. *RLG Preservation Microfilming Handbook*. Mountain View, Ca.: Research Libraries Group, 1992.

European Register of Microform Masters [EROMM]/Catalogue Europeen de Microformes Meres. N.p.: n.p., 1993. Offprint.

Facts on File: World News Digest with Index. 1993 issues.

Fang, Josephine Riss, and Ann Russell, eds. *Education and Training for Preservation and Conservation*. (IFLA Publications 54) München: K.G. Saur, 1991.

Farr, George F., Jr. "NEH's Program for the Preservation of Brittle Books." In *Advances in Preservation and Access*, ed. by Barbra Buckner Higginbotham and Mary E. Jackson, 49-60. Westport, Conn.: Meckler, 1992.

Feather, John. *Guidelines for the Teaching of Preservation to Librarians, Archivists and Documentalists for a Joint Working Party of IFLA's Sections on Conservation and Education and Training*. N.p., 1988-89?

---. "National and International Policies for Preservation." *International Library Review* 20 (1990): 315-327.

---, and Anne Lusher. "Education for Conservation in British Library Schools: Current Practices and Future Prospects." *Journal of Librarianship* 21.2 (April 1989): 129-138.

---, ---. *The Teaching of Conservation in LIS Schools in Great Britain*. (British Library Research Paper 49.) London: The British Library, 1988.

Fiddes, R.G., and D.R. Winterbottom. *The Feasibility of Electronic Accession of Archive Material at the Printers*. British Library R & D Report 6061. [London]: British Library Research and Development Department, 1991.

Fitch, James Marston. *Historic Preservation: Curatorial Management of the Built World.* New York: McGraw Hill, 1982; rpt. Charlottesville and London: University of Virginia Press, 1990.

Follett, Mary Parker. "The Giving of Orders." In H.C. Metcalf and L. Urwick, eds., *Dynamic Administration: The Collected Papers of Mary Parker Follett*, pp. 58-59. New York: Harper & Bros., 1942.

Fredericks, Maria. "Recent Trends in Book Conservation and Library Collections Care." *Journal of the American Institute for Conservation* 31.1 (Spring 1992): 95-101.

Getty Conservation Institute. *Training Program Activities 1985-1991.* Marina del Rey, CA: Getty Conservation Institute, February 1991.

Greene, Virginia. "'Accessories of Holiness': Defining Jewish Sacred Objects." *Journal of the American Institute for Conservation.* 31.1 (Spring 1992): 31-39.

Grenot, Teresa Lupe. "Distance Education For Preservation Training and Continuing Education." Unpublished paper, April 1993.

Gwinn, Nancy E., ed. *Preservation Microfilming: A Guide for Librarians and Archivists.* Chicago and London: American Library Association, 1987.

Hammer, John H. "On the Political Aspects of Book Preservation in the U.S." In *Advances in Preservation and Access*, ed. by Barbra Buckner Higginbotham and Mary E. Jackson, 22-40. Westport, Conn.: Meckler, 1992.

Hannigan, Jane Anne. "Distance Learning and Interactivity." In *Project Century 21: A Research and Action Program for Meeting the Information Needs of Society. Background Papers.* Chicago: American Library Association, President's Committee on Project Century 21, 1993, pp. 19-42.

Havemann, Joel. "'Mafia Terror'" Blamed in Blast at Italy Museum." *Los Angeles Times,* May 28, 1993, A1.

"Help for Conservation in Less Developed Countries." *Abbey Newsletter: Bookbinding and Conservation.* 16.4 (August 1992): 64.

Higginbotham, Barbra Buckner. *Our Past Preserved: A History of American Library Preservation, 1876-1910.* Boston: G.K. Hall, 1990.

---, and Mary E. Jackson, eds. *Advances in Preservation and Access.* Vol. 1. Westport, Conn.: Meckler, 1992.

Horton, Carolyn. *Cleaning and Preserving Bindings and Related Materials.* Library Technology Program No. 12. Chicago: American Library Association, 1967; 2nd ed., LTP No. 16, 1969.

Hovy, Eduard. "How MT Works." *BYTE 18.1* (January 1993): 167-176.

Hughes, Robert. "Striking at the Past Itself." *Time,* June 7, 1993, 34-35.

Image Permanence Institute. *Storage Guide for Acetate Film.* Rochester, N.Y.: Rochester Institute of Technology, Image Permanence Institute, 1993.

"International Book Bank." *Abbey Newsletter: Bookbinding and Conservation* 16.6 (November 1992): 81- 82.

International Council of Museums. Committee for Conservation. *The Graduate Conservator in Employment: Expectations and Realities.* (Proceedings of the Interim Meeting of the Working Group on Training in Conservation and Restoration of the ICOM Committee for Conservation. Amsterdam and Leiden, 31 August - 1 September, 1989.) Amsterdam: International Council Of Museums. Committee for Conservation, 1990.

International Federation of Library Associations and Institutions. *IFLA Annual 1988. Proceedings of the 54th General Conference, Sydney, Australia.* München: K.G. Saur, 1989.

---. *IFLA Annual* 1989. *Proceedings of the 55th General Conference, Paris, France, 1989.* München: K.G. Saur, 1990.

---. *IFLA Annual 1990. Proceedings of the 56th General Conference, Stockholm, Sweden, 1990.* München: K.G. Saur, 1991.

---. *IFLA Annual 1991. Proceedings of the 57th General Conference, Moscow, Russia, 1991.* München: K.G. Saur, 1992.

International Index on Training in Conservation of Cultural Property/Répertoire international des institutions donnant une formation pour la conservation des biens culturels. Rome: ICCROM and Marina del Rey, CA: The Getty Conservation Institute, 1987. [New edition in press, Getty Conservation Institute. Projected for 1994.]

Kastaly, Beatrix. "Preservation and Conservation of Library Materials in Hungary." *Conservation Administration News* 41 (April 1990): 1, 2, 30.

Kathpalia, Y.P. *A Model Curriculum for the Training of Specialists in Document Preservation and Restoration: A Ramp Study with Guidelines.* (PGI-84/WS/2) Paris: Unesco, 1984.

Kenney, Anne R. "Digital-to-Microfilm Conversion: An Interim Preservation Solution." *Library Resources & Technical Services* 37.4 (October 1993): 380-401.

Kenney, Anne R. and Lynne K. Personius. *Update on Digital Techniques*. Insert in *The Commission on Preservation and Access Newsletter* 40 (November-December, 1991): 1-6.

Kimmelman, Michael. "After Bombing, the Uffizi Begins Recovery." *New York Times,* June 17, 1993, B1, B4.

---. "Ruined Works Stand as Symbols of Vulnerability." *New York Times,* May 28, 1993, A8.

Kurzweil, Raymond. "The Future of Libraries. Part 1: The Technology of the Book." *Library Journal* 117.1 (January 1992): 80, 82.

---. "The Future of Libraries. Part 2: The End of Books." *Library Journal* 117.3 (February 15, 1992): 140-141.

---. "The Future of Libraries. Part 3: The Virtual Library." *Library Journal* 117.5 (March 15, 1992): 63-64.

Lancaster, F. Wilfrid. "What Has UNESCO Achieved in Education and Training for the Information Professions?" *Journal of Education for Library and Information Science* 32.1-2 (Summer/Fall 1991): 69-76.

Large, Andrew. "Curriculum Development: Some Reflections on UNESCO's Role." *Journal of Education for Library and Information Science* 32.1-2 (Summer/Fall 1991): 77-83.

Larkin, Philip. *Collected Poems*. Ed. by Anthony Thwaite. New York: Farrar, Straus, Giroux; London: Marvell Press, 1989.

Lesk, Michael. *Preservation of New Technology*. Washington, D.C.: Commission on Preservation and Access, 1992.

Malinconico, S. Michael. "What Librarians Need to Know to Survive in an Age of Technology." *Journal of Education for Library and Information Science* 33.3 (Summer 1992): 226-240.

Maynor, Catherine I. "Publications of the AIC Book and Paper Group." *Journal of the American Institute for Conservation* 31.1 (Spring 1992): 103-106.

McClung, Patricia A. "Consortial Action: RLG's Preservation Program." In *Advances in Preservation and Access*, ed. by Barbra Buckner Higginbothan and Mary E. Jackson, 61-70. Westport, Conn.: Meckler, 1992.

Middleton, Bernard C. *The Restoration of Leather Bindings*. Library Technology Program Publication No. 18. Chicago: American Library Association, 1972.

Miller, L. Chris. "Babelware for the Desktop." *BYTE* 18.1 (January 1993): 177-186.

Moravcsik, Michael J. *Science Development: The Building of Science in Less Developed Countries*. N.P.: Program for Advanced Studies in Institution Building and Technical Assistance Methodology, 1976.

Mostafavi, Mohsen, and David Leatherbarrow. *On Weathering: The Life of Buildings in Time*. Cambridge, MA: MIT Press, 1993.

Naisbitt, John. *Megatrends: Ten New Directions Transforming Our Lives*. New York: Warner Books, 1982.

---, and Patricia Aburdene. *Megatrends 2000: Ten New Directions for the 1990s*. New York: William Morrow, 1990.

National Information Standards Organization. *Permanence of Paper for Publications and Documents in Libraries and Archives* (ANSI/NISO Z39.48-1992). New Brunswick, N.J.: Transaction Publishers, 1993.

National Preservation News. No. 1, July 1985 - No. 8, October 1987.

Noguiera, Carmen C., ed. *Glossary of Basic Archival and Library Conservation Terms*. (English with equivalents in Spanish, German, Italian, French and Russian.) Compiled by the Committee on Conservation, International Council on Archives. München: K.G. Saur, 1988.

Patterson, Robert H. "Columbia's Institute & CAN." *Conservation Administration News* no. 1 (June 1979): 3.

Pelzman, Frankie. "And What Did You Think of WHCLIS II?" *Wilson Library Bulletin* 66.9 (May 1992): 21-22.

"Post-Graduate Programmes in Information Science." *UNISIST Newsletter* 19.3 (1991): 50-51.

Preservation and Conservation of Library Documents: A UNESCO/IFLA/ICA Enquiry into the Current State of the World's Patrimony. (PGI-87/WS/15) Paris: UNESCO, 1987.

Preservation Education Task Force. *Report*. Washington, D.C.: Comission on Preservation and Access, August 1, 1991.

Preservation Policy. National Information Services and Responsibilities. Permanence and Durability of Information Products. In *ALA Handbook, 1992-93.* Chicago: American Library Association, 1993, 145.

Public Papers of the Presidents of the United States. George Bush, 1990. Book II, July 1 to December 31, 1990. Washington, D.C.: GPO, 1991.

Raphael, Bettina. "Preventive Conservation in Latin America." *Abbey Newsletter* 17.5 (October 1993): 67.

Ratcliffe, F.W. *Preservation Policies and Conservation in British Libraries.* (Library and Information Research Report no. 25) Wetherby, West Yorkshire: British Library, 1984.

Ratcliffe, Fred. "Education in Preservation for Librarians and Conservators." *Library Association Record* 88.10 (October 1986): 493, 495, 497.

Ray, Eric, with Joel Lurie Grishaver. *Sofer: The Story of a Torah Scroll.* Los Angeles: Torah Aura Productions, 1986.

Roberts, Barbara O. "Establishing a Disaster Prevention/Response Plan: An International Perspective & Assessment." *Technology & Conservation* 11.4 (Winter 1992-93): 15-17, 35, 36.

Rütimann, Hans. *The International Project.* (Progress Report) Washington, D.C.: Commission on Preservation and Access, August 1989.

---. *The International Project 1992 Update Including "Microfilming Projects Abroad."* Washington, D.C.: Commission on Preservation and Access, January 1993.

---. *Preservation and Access in China: Report of the Final Visit to the People's Republic of China September 19 to October 12, 1991.* Washington, D.C.: Commission on Preservation and Access, March 1992.

Sack, Susanne P. "In Memoriam: A Tribute to Sheldon Keck." *AIC News* 18.5 (September 1993): 18-19.

Skepastianu, Maria. "Preservation and Conservation Education in Greece." *Conservation Administration News* 50 (July 1992): 8, 9, 26, 27.

Slow Fires: On the Preservation of the Human Record. Terry Sanders, producer/distributor. VHS 3/4-inch cassette, 16mm film; 60-minute or 30-minute versions. Santa Monica, California, 1988.

Smith, Merrily A. "The Dissemination of Preservation Information," in *Managing the Preservation of Serial Literature: An International Symposium, Conference Held at the Library of Congress, Washington, D.C., May 22-24, 1989.* Ed. by Merrily A. Smith. (IFLA Publications 57) München: K.G. Saur, 1992.

---. "The IFLA Core Programme on Preservation and Conservation (PAC)." *IFLA Journal* 12.4 (1986): 305-06.

---. "Preservation Education in Library Schools." In *Preservation of Library Materials: Conference Held at the National Library of Austria, Vienna, April 7-10, 1986*, 11-18. Ed. by Merrily A. Smith. 2 vols. (IFLA Publications 40-41) München: K.G. Saur, 1987.

Sniffen, Michael J. "Lost in Tapes: History Fades as Computer Efforts Focus on Future. *Louisville Courier-Journal* (January 2, 1991); rpt. *Abbey Newsletter* 15.3 (May 1991): 46-47.

Soloway, Elliot, et al. "Reading and Writing in the 21st Century." EDUCOM Review 28.1 (January/February 1993): 26-29.

Stam, David. "Statement of David H. Stam University Librarian, Syracuse University, Speaking on Behalf of The Association of Research Libraries, The Commission on Preservation and Access, and the National Humanities Alliance On the Fiscal Year 1994 Appropriations for the National Endowment for the Humanities Before the Subcommittee on the Interior and Related Agencies, Committee on Appropriations, U.S. House of Representatives, May 12, 1993." Unpublished version.

Steele, Victoria and Stephen D. Elder. *Becoming a Fundraiser: The Principles and Practice of Library Development.* Chicago: American Library Association, 1992.

Stevenson, Condict Gaye. *Working Together: Case Studies in Cooperative Preservation.* Washington, D.C.: Commission on Preservation and Access, September 1991.

Stielow, Frederick J. "Biting the WORM: Theory and Tales of Electronic Media Preservation. *Conservation Administration News* 47 (October 1991): 10.

St-Laurent, Gilles. *The Care and Handling of Recorded Sound Materials.* Washington, D.C.: Commission on Preservation and Access, 1991.

Stobart, Janet. "Pope, Italy's Chief Mourn Bomb Victims." *Los Angeles Times*, July 29, 1993, A1, A9.

Stratton, John B. "Libraries and Commercial Binderies." *Library Trends* 4.3 (January 1956): 301-311.

Swartzburg, Susan G. "Resources for the Conservation of Southeast Asian Art." *Art Libraries Journal* 18.2 (1993): 39-43.

Swartzburg, Susan Garretson. "Preservation Education for Librarians: Some Thoughts." In *Education and Training for Preservation and Conservation . . .*, 86-89. Ed. by Josephine Riss Fang and Ann Russell. München: K.G. Saur, 1991.

---, and Robert E. Schnare. "Programs and Issues in Preservation for the 1990s: A Bibliographic Overview." In *Advances in Preservation and Access*, ed. by Barbra Buckner Higginbotham and Mary E. Jackson, 262-282. Westport, Conn.: Meckler, 1992.

Tanselle, G. Thomas. "Reproductions and Scholarship." *Studies in Bibliography* 42 (1989): 25-54.

Tauber, Maurice, ed. *Conservation of Library Materials. Library Trends* 4.3 (January 1956): 215-334.

United States Statutes at Large, 1990. Vol. 104, Pt. 1, Public Laws 101-241 through 101-440. Washington, D.C.: GPO, 1991.

Vasconcellos, Muriel. "Machine Translation." *BYTE* 18.1 (January 1993): 153-164.

Vivarelli, Niccolo. "Blood and Masterpieces: A Car Bomb Shatters Italy's Uffizi Gallery." *Newsweek*, June 7, 1993, 32.

Vodosek, Peter. "The Internationalization of Information: Impact of the European Community on Library and Information Science Studies in Germany." *Journal of Education for Library and Information Science* 34.4 (Fall 1993): 314-316.

Waters, Donald, and Shari Weaver. *The Organizational Phase of Project Open Book.* Washington, D.C.: Commission on Preservation and Access, September 1992.

Waters, Peter. *Procedures for Salvage of Water-Damaged Library Materials*. 2nd ed. Washington, D.C.: Library of Congress, 1979.

Wellheiser, Johanna G. *Nonchemical Treatment Processes for Disinfestation of Insects and Fungi in Library Collections.* (IFLA Publications 60) München: K.G. Saur, 1992.

White House Conference on Library and Information Services (WHCLIS). *Information 2000: Library and Information Services for the 21st Century.* Washington, D.C.: U.S. G.P.O., 1991.

Williams, Gordon. *The Preservation of Deteriorating Books: An Examination of the Problem with Recommendations for a Solution.* Washington, D.C.: Association of Research Libraries, 1964.

Wilson, Alexander. *Library Policy for Preservation and Conservation in the European Community: Principles, Practices and the Contribution of New Information Technologies.* (Commission of the European Communities) München: K.G. Saur, 1988.

Yearbook of International Organizations, 1992/1993. 29th ed. München: K.G. Saur, 1993.

Zappalà, Antonio. "Instruction in 'Book Restoration' in the Graduate Course in *Conservation of Cultural Property* at the University of Udine, Italy." *Restaurator* 9.1 (1988): 27-36.

INDEX